Grilling gone wild

ZESTY RECIPES FOR MEATS, MAINS, MARINADES & MORE!!

FOX CHAPEL
PUBLISHING

© 2012 by Fox Chapel Publishing Company, Inc., 1970 Broad Street, East Petersburg, PA 17520

Recipe selection, design, and book design © Fox Chapel Publishing.
Recipes and photography © G&R Publishing DBA CQ Products.

ISBN 978-1-56523-725-4

Library of Congress Cataloging-in-Publication Data

Couch, Peg.
 Grilling gone wild : zesty recipes for meats, mains, marinades, and more / Peg Couch.
    p. cm.
 Includes index.
 ISBN 978-1-56523-725-4 (pbk.)
 1. Barbecuing. 2. Grilling (Cooking) I. Title.
 TX840.B3C676 2012
 641.7'6--dc23
                          2011052421

To learn more about the other great books from Fox Chapel Publishing, or to find a retailer near you,
call toll free 800-457-9112 or visit us at *www.FoxChapelPublishing.com*.

Note to Authors: We are always looking for talented authors to write new books. Please send a brief letter describing your idea to Acquisition Editor, 1970 Broad Street, East Petersburg, PA 17520.

Printed in China
First printing

At its heart, grilling is a simple and approachable way to cook: Grab a piece of meat or vegetable, put it over flames, and flip periodically until it's cooked. You can grill up perfectly good food in just that way. But when you take the time to add a little something extra—a rub, marinade, sauce, salsa, or glaze—you can transform a meal that's just good into something deliciously unexpected. This book teaches you how to pump up the flavor by first showing how to prepare a basic version of each meat or vegetable, and then providing recipes that build off the basics. Chapters for poultry, beef, pork, seafood, vegetables, and fruits will give you ideas and inspiration to craft an entire meal from the grill. With the hundreds of recipes in these pages at your disposal, before long you'll be a grilling master. Happy grilling!

CONTENTS

BEEF   46

PORK

SEAFOOD

VEGETABLES   100

FRUITS 131

INDEX 147

GETTING STARTED

WILD & WONDERFUL GRILLING TIPS

- Preheat a gas grill for 10 to 15 minutes before cooking. If using charcoal briquettes, light them and allow briquettes to turn white before placing food on the grate. (It will take approximately 20 to 30 minutes.)

- Clean the grates with a wire brush before cooking. This is especially important when cooking delicate foods, such as seafood or ground chicken patties.

- To prevent food from sticking to the grate, dip a folded paper towel in canola oil and rub it over grates until lightly coated with oil. If spraying grates with nonstick cooking spray, do it before lighting the grill. You may also brush meat and seafood lightly with olive oil before grilling.

- If making kebabs or grilling small pieces of food, thread food on metal skewers, or use wooden skewers that have been soaked in water for 15 to 30 minutes to prevent scorching. The food will twist less if threaded on a pair of skewers.

- Trim off excess fat from steaks, chops and roasts before grilling to prevent flare-ups. Cut off excess poultry skin before marinating or cooking.

- Mix seasonings into ground meats before grilling, using hands as needed.

- When making ground meat patties, gently shape the meat with a fork to avoid compressing the meat too firmly.

- Use a spatula or tongs to turn meats such as chicken breasts or steaks. Avoid forks, which pierce the meat and cause juices to run out.

- Soaking meats in a brine or marinade will increase flavor and juiciness.

- If basting meats with melted butter, avoid flare-ups by grilling one side first and turning the meat over before brushing with butter.

REMEMBER THESE FOOD SAFETY TIPS

Wash hands and cutting boards thoroughly after handling raw meat or poultry, and never place cooked meats on the same surface previously used to hold raw meats unless it has been washed well.

On picnics, use well-insulated coolers and ice packs to keep foods cold and prevent bacteria growth before and after cooking (40° or below).

Serve grilled foods hot and chill leftovers as soon as the meal is over.

MARINADE & BRINE HOW-TOS

Marinades and brines add flavor, moisture and tenderness to meats and seafood before grilling. If you wish to brush meat with some of the marinade during grilling, it is best to reserve a portion of the mixture before using the remaining mixture to soak raw meat. Marinade that has been in contact with raw meat may contain bacteria that could contaminate the cooked meat. The used marinade should be boiled for at least 3 minutes before being used on cooked meat.

There are two good methods to marinate meat and seafood. For quick clean-ups, place the food in a large heavy-duty resealable plastic bag resting in a large bowl. Pour the marinade over the food, seal the bag and gently turn it until meat or seafood is well coated. Alternatively, use a non-reactive container, such as a shallow glass baking dish or stainless steel or plastic bowl (never aluminum). Place the meat in the container, pour marinade over the top, turn the pieces several times until well coated and then cover the dish. Always refrigerate meat or seafood while it marinates and turn it several times to incorporate flavors.

To cook, remove food from the plastic bag or dish and discard the marinade. Do not rinse off the marinade, but if the meat seems too wet, pat off the excess with paper towels. This prevents the marinade from dripping into the grill and causing flare-ups. Use the fresh reserved marinade to baste the meat or seafood as it cooks. Reserved marinade can also be served alongside the grilled food.

Marinades with an acidic ingredient, like vinegar, wine or citrus juice, help tenderize meat or seafood. Avoid marinades with too many sweet ingredients as they can cause the meat to burn.

Brines are typically salty soaks and are not used for basting or serving. Always discard the brine after soaking is complete, and rinse the meat before grilling to remove excess salt. Though brining will shorten the cooking time, it turns pork and beef gray in color, so it's best to grill meat thoroughly for a nicely browned appearance.

RUB HOW-TOS

Dry rubs are combinations of spices and seasonings without any wet ingredients. These rubs increase a meat's natural browning. Wet rubs are paste-like because oil or another wet ingredient is mixed in with the spices and seasonings to create a crust.

Apply a rub 15 to 20 minutes before grilling so the seasonings can penetrate into the meat. Sprinkle the rub mixture over the meat or seafood and gently pat or massage it in with your fingers. Avoid rubbing the mixture into the meat too vigorously.

Standard rub seasonings include salt and pepper. For best results, choose coarse kosher salt, which won't create a wet surface on meat like table salt can, and use freshly ground black pepper, whose oils offer a deeper flavor. Brown sugar will add more flavor than white sugar in sweet rubs.

If meat has been soaked in a brine or salty marinade, rinse the meat and use a salt-free rub before grilling.

SALSA & RELISH HOW-TOS

Salsas and relishes made from fruits or vegetables add color, flavor and texture to grilled dishes. When served chilled, they also offer a nice temperature contrast. Whether chunky or almost smooth, salsas and relishes can be spooned on top or served alongside grilled poultry, beef, pork or seafood. Choose fresh seasonal ingredients that complement the flavor of the grilled meat or seafood.

SAUCE & GLAZE HOW-TOS

Sauces and glazes are used to baste meats as they cook on the grill, and they can also be served over grilled dishes. If there is a high sugar content in the sauce or glaze, wait until the end of the cooking time before brushing the meat with it. This prevents burning and allows the sauce to caramelize before serving. If using the mixture as both a basting sauce and finishing sauce, you must boil it for several minutes before serving. A "mop" is a thin barbeque sauce brushed on food like ribs during grilling. It adds flavor and keeps food moist.

WOOD CHIP & SMOKING HOW-TOS

To get a smoked flavor in grilled meats, add fully dried (not green) wood chunks or chips to the charcoal or gas grill before cooking. Fruit woods, such as apple, plum or cherry, complement turkey. Hickory is a good choice for almost any type of meat, especially pork. Mesquite works well if used sparingly. Wood chunks tend to smolder rather than burn, which produces steadier smoke than chips. Never use treated lumber scraps or wood from high-sap trees like pine or fir, though cedar planks can be used to smoke salmon on the grill.

Soak one or two handfuls of the wood in water for 1 hour and then drain well. In a charcoal grill, place the damp wood directly on the briquettes, around the outer edges. In either a charcoal or gas grill, wood can also be placed in a smoke box, small disposable foil pan or a heavy-duty foil pouch poked full of holes. Set this container on the lava rocks in a gas grill or directly on the charcoal before preheating, locating it near the back or to one side of the grill. When the grill is hot and smoke is produced, reduce the grill's temperature and place meat on the grate away from the smoke. (Never place meat directly over the smoke.) Close the lid and let the smoke seep into the meat as it cooks. If food requires a long grilling time, add more wood as needed, especially during the first two hours of cooking.

TEMPERATURE GUIDE FOR GRILLED MEATS

Meats and seafood should be cooked thoroughly for safe eating. Cooking times in the recipes are approximate. The time required may vary due to the size and shape of the food, personal preferences and the weather. In cool or windy weather, it may be necessary to cook food longer.

Use of an instant-read thermometer can prevent under- or over-cooking. Insert it in the thickest part of the cut to obtain an accurate reading. Though all meats and seafood must be grilled to safe minimum internal temperatures before serving, you may prefer to cook some cuts to a higher temperature. However, over-cooking causes meat and seafood to dry out. Remember that foods will continue to cook for a few minutes after being removed from the grill.

Revised USDA guidelines recommend cooking foods to the following minimum internal temperatures to kill harmful food bacteria.

Tender or thin cuts of meat can be placed directly over higher heat to be grilled quickly (less than 30 minutes). Cuts of meat that are tougher or larger need to be cooked more slowly, using lower temperatures and moisture to become tender. It is also helpful to soak these cuts in a tenderizing marinade before grilling.

Many meats benefit from resting or standing time. After removing meat from the grill, cover with a foil tent and let stand for 5 to 15 minutes before slicing. This allows the internal temperature to rise adequately and juices to redistribute throughout the meat.

Meat	Temperature
Fish	145°
Beef Roasts and Steaks	145° (rare)
	160° (medium)
	170° (well-done)
Ground Beef and Ground Pork	160°
Pork Chops, Tenderloins, Roasts	160°
Ground Poultry	165°
Chicken Breasts	165° (up to 170°)
Chicken or Turkey Thighs, Legs, Quarters, Whole Birds	165° (up to 180°)

GAS GRILLS VS. CHARCOAL GRILLS

Most meats and main dishes can be cooked equally well on a gas or charcoal grill. Convenience and personal preference will help you choose. Grilling food with the lid on enhances the grilled flavor and shortens the cooking time, even with a slightly lower temperature. If cooking on a charcoal grill without a lid, you may need to increase the temperature and cooking time slightly.

Certain recipes require a tight-fitting lid, such as smoked or slow-cooked meats. The smoke and heat must be held inside to properly cook these foods.

Thermometers are available to judge the temperature inside a grill. Gas grills usually have a built-in temperature gauge with dials to regulate the heat and number of burners turned on, but check the accuracy of the gauge before relying on it. A barbeque-safe oven thermometer may be more accurate.

The temperature of a charcoal grill can be regulated by the number of hot briquettes used or the placement of the grate. Use fewer coals to reduce the heat, or add more briquettes to make it hotter. Move the grate of the grill closer to the coals to increase the temperature or further away for less heat.

DIRECT HEAT VS. INDIRECT HEAT

When food is placed on the grate right over the heat source, it will cook quickly by direct heat. This is best for small, tender foods that can be cooked in less than 30 minutes. The grill does not need a lid unless otherwise directed.

To cook foods more slowly, use indirect heat. This is accomplished by heating only one section of the grill and placing the food on the grate over the remaining cooler section before closing the lid. The heat will circulate inside the grill to cook the food slowly at a lower temperature ("low and slow"). Avoid opening the lid to peek at the food. It is best to use a thermometer to measure the temperature inside the grill when cooking this way.

To lock in the juices of larger cuts of meat, sear all sides over hot direct heat for 1 to 2 minutes per side. Then reduce the heat, close the lid and move the food on the grate as needed to finish cooking over direct or indirect heat.

Flare-ups occur when fat drips on the heat source. To extinguish flames on a charcoal grill, squirt water on them. On gas grill, don't use water; just close the lid and vents to cut off the air source.

Placing an aluminum drip pan (holding a small amount of water) in the bottom of the grill also reduces flare-ups and provides moisture for indirect cooking. The pan should be set underneath the cooking area, with heat surrounding the pan.

After cooking on any grill, burn off residue on the grates and when cool, scrape off baked-on food before putting the grill away.

POULTRY

BASIC COOKING TIPS

Fully cooked poultry should reach the internal temperatures listed below, as shown by a thermometer. Grilled chicken or turkey is generally done when the meat is no longer pink inside and the juices run clear when sliced in the thickest part.

	Cook to
Boneless skinless chicken breast halves & tenders	165° to 170°
Chicken parts: wings, legs, thighs, quarters	165° to 180°
Whole chicken	165° to 180°
Boneless skinless turkey tenderloin steaks	165° to 170°
Turkey drumsticks	165° to 180°
Ground chicken & turkey	165°

To stuff chicken breast halves, butterfly each piece by slicing it horizontally from the thickest part toward the thinnest part, stopping about ¼" from the edge. Open it up and pat gently to make one large flat piece. Roll it around a stuffing or filling. Chicken breasts may also be pounded flatter with the smooth side of a meat mallet and simply folded in half around a stuffing. Secure both with toothpicks to contain stuffing. Stuffed chicken breasts may take slightly longer to cook.

CHICKEN BREAST HALVES

Boneless skinless chicken breast halves cook quickly on a grill, but cooking time depends on the size and thickness of each piece. Generally, if using medium direct heat, they will need approximately 12 to 15 minutes, turning once partway through cooking. If using indirect heat, allow about 5 minutes longer.

BASIC GRILLED CHICKEN BREASTS

Makes 4 servings

4 boneless skinless chicken breast halves
1 (16 oz.) bottle Italian salad dressing
Lemon pepper to taste
Salt to taste

Rinse chicken breast halves and pat dry. Place chicken in a large resealable plastic bag and pour salad dressing over the chicken. Seal bag and turn several times to coat meat. Refrigerate bag to marinate chicken for 2 to 3 hours, turning twice to marinate evenly.

To cook, lightly oil the grate and preheat grill to medium heat. Remove chicken breasts from bag and discard marinade. Arrange chicken on the grate directly over heat and season with lemon pepper and salt. Cook for 12 to 15 minutes, turning once halfway through cooking and adjusting heat as needed for even grilling. When meat is no longer pink and juices run clear, place chicken breasts on a serving plate and cover with foil to rest for 5 to 10 minutes, allowing internal temperature to reach 165° to 170° before serving.

CAJUN RUB

Makes about 1 tablespoon

1 tsp. black pepper
½ tsp. white pepper
½ tsp. cayenne pepper
½ tsp. salt
½ tsp. ground cumin
½ tsp. ground nutmeg
Vegetable oil for brushing

In a small bowl, combine black pepper, white pepper, cayenne pepper, salt, cumin and nutmeg; mix well. Lightly brush both sides of chicken breast halves with vegetable oil and sprinkle rub mixture on top, rubbing it gently into meat. Grill chicken as directed above.

Replace Italian dressing, lemon pepper and salt in the Basic Grilled Chicken Breasts above with one of these rubs before grilling.

SPICE RUB

Makes about ⅓ cup

3 T. paprika
1 T. ground cumin
1 T. dry mustard
2 tsp. ground fennel seeds
1 tsp. salt
1 tsp. black pepper
Canola oil for brushing

In a small bowl, combine paprika, cumin, dry mustard, fennel, salt and pepper; mix well. Lightly brush both sides of each chicken breast half with canola oil. Rub the top of each piece with spice mixture and place on a lightly oiled grate over direct heat, rub side down; cook for 4 to 5 minutes or until golden brown and crusty. Turn chicken over and continue to grill for 10 minutes or until cooked through.

MARINADE WITH A KICK

Marinates 4 chicken breast halves

½ C. cider vinegar
¼ C. vegetable oil
2½ tsp. Worcestershire sauce
2 tsp. hot pepper sauce
1 tsp. salt

In a small bowl, whisk together vinegar, oil, Worcestershire sauce, hot pepper sauce and salt. Set aside ¼ cup of the marinade for basting during grilling; cover and refrigerate. Pour remaining mixture over chicken and refrigerate to marinate meat for 4 hours. To cook, drain and discard marinade. Grill chicken as directed on page 15, using the reserved marinade to baste meat several times toward the end of cooking.

CITRUS MARINADE

Marinates 4 chicken breast halves

½ C. orange juice
¼ C. lime juice
¼ C. lemon juice
1 T. olive oil
1 tsp. chopped fresh basil
½ tsp. salt
¼ tsp. black pepper

In a small bowl, combine orange, lime and lemon juices, oil, basil, salt and black pepper; mix well. Pour juice mixture over chicken and refrigerate to marinate meat for 3 to 4 hours, turning occasionally. To cook, drain and discard marinade. Grill chicken as directed on page 15.

In place of the Italian salad dressing marinade in the Basic Grilled Chicken Breasts on page 15, try one of these marinades. Marinate chicken in a large resealable plastic bag or shallow glass baking dish in the refrigerator.

ORIENTAL MARINADE

Marinates 4 chicken breast halves

- ½ C. olive oil
- ½ C. white grape juice
- ½ C. reduced-sodium soy sauce
- ½ C. chopped green onion
- 3 T. sesame seeds, toasted*
- 1 T. dry mustard
- 1 T. grated fresh gingerroot
- 1 tsp. black pepper
- 4 cloves garlic, minced

In a large resealable plastic bag, combine oil, grape juice, soy sauce, green onion, sesame seeds, dry mustard, gingerroot, black pepper and garlic; mix well. Set aside ½ cup of sauce for basting during grilling; cover and refrigerate. Add chicken to remaining mixture in bag, seal and turn bag to coat meat; refrigerate bag to marinate chicken for 4 to 6 hours. To cook, drain and discard marinade. Grill chicken as directed on page 15, using the reserved marinade to baste meat several times toward the end of cooking.

* To toast, place sesame seeds in a dry skillet over medium heat and cook until browned, about 3 to 5 minutes, shaking pan often.

TROPICAL MARINADE

Marinates 4 chicken breast halves

- ½ C. pineapple juice
- 2 T. apricot preserves
- 1 tsp. ground ginger
- 1 tsp. dry mustard
- ½ tsp. salt

In a small bowl, whisk together pineapple juice, preserves, ginger, dry mustard and salt until well blended. Pour mixture over chicken and refrigerate to marinate meat for 3 to 4 hours, turning occasionally. To cook, drain and discard marinade. Grill chicken as directed on page 15.

To make Hawaiian Chicken & Pineapple Sandwiches: *Spread Thousand Island dressing on split, toasted onion rolls and top each roll with one grilled chicken breast prepared with Tropical Marinade, a grilled pineapple ring and slice of Swiss cheese.*

PERFECTLY SMOKED MARINADE

Marinates 4 chicken breast halves

- ⅔ C. olive oil
- ⅔ C. reduced sodium soy sauce
- ¼ C. lemon juice
- 2 T. liquid smoke flavoring
- 2 T. Dijon mustard
- 2 tsp. black pepper
- 2 tsp. garlic powder

In a small bowl, mix together oil, soy sauce, lemon juice, liquid smoke, Dijon mustard, black pepper and garlic powder; mix well. Pour marinade over chicken and refrigerate to marinate meat for 3 to 4 hours, turning occasionally. To cook, drain and discard marinade. Grill chicken as directed on page 15.

LEMON MARINADE

Marinates 4 chicken breast halves

⅓ C. lemon juice
¼ C. olive oil
2 to 3 tsp. Dijon mustard
2 cloves garlic, minced
2 T. finely chopped red bell pepper
½ tsp. salt
¼ tsp. black pepper

In a small bowl, combine lemon juice, oil, Dijon mustard, garlic, bell pepper, salt and black pepper; mix well. Set aside ¼ cup of the mixture for basting during grilling; cover and refrigerate. Pour remaining mixture over chicken and refrigerate to marinate meat for at least 20 minutes. Grill chicken as directed on page 15, using the reserved marinade to baste meat several times toward the end of cooking.

This marinade also tastes good with chicken tenders.

RED PEPPER RELISH

Garnishes 4 to 8 chicken breast halves

1½ large red bell pepper, finely chopped
⅓ C. finely chopped onion
¼ C. sugar
¼ C. cider vinegar
½ tsp. salt
¼ tsp. crushed red pepper flakes, or to taste

In a small saucepan over medium heat, combine bell pepper, onion, sugar, vinegar, salt and red pepper flakes. Bring mixture to a boil, reduce heat and simmer uncovered for 20 minutes or until most of the liquid has evaporated and vegetables are tender. Let relish cool slightly before spooning into an airtight container. Chill before serving alongside grilled chicken breasts. Relish may be refrigerated for up to 2 weeks.

Red Pepper Relish also tastes good on burgers and hot dogs.

ORANGE BBQ SAUCE

Makes about ⅔ cup

½ C. barbeque sauce of choice
½ tsp. grated orange peel
2 T. orange juice

In a small bowl, stir together barbeque sauce, orange peel and orange juice until blended. After grilling chicken breast halves on one side as directed on page 15, turn them over and brush generously with Orange-BBQ Sauce. Continue to cook, brushing with sauce again before serving.

Prepare Basic Grilled Chicken Breasts on page 15 without the Italian salad dressing marinade but use these sauces to baste the chicken during grilling time.

HONEYED TANGERINE GLAZE

Makes about ½ cup

3 C. tangerine juice or tangerine-
   orange juice
5 sprigs fresh thyme
¼ C. honey
½ tsp. salt
¼ tsp. black pepper

In a medium saucepan over high heat, combine tangerine juice and thyme. Bring mixture to a boil and cook, stirring frequently, until thickened and reduced to about ½ cup. Remove and discard thyme stems. Whisk in honey until well blended; season with salt and black pepper. Transfer to a bowl and cool glaze to room temperature. To use, grill one side of chicken breast halves (plain or pre-coated with Spice Rub on page 16) for 6 to 8 minutes. Turn chicken over and cook for 2 to 3 more minutes. Brush with glaze and continue to cook until almost done. Turn again, brush tops with glaze and finish grilling.

PEPPER-JACK STUFFING

Fills 4 chicken breast halves

¼ tsp. salt
¼ tsp. black pepper
4 slices Monterey Jack cheese with
   jalapeno peppers
1 T. butter, melted
½ C. chunky salsa

Lightly oil the grate and preheat grill to medium heat. Butterfly four chicken breast halves as directed on page 14. Sprinkle chicken with the salt and black pepper. Cut cheese slices as needed to fit in the center of each chicken piece. Roll chicken around the cheese, folding in sides to enclose cheese; secure with toothpicks. Place chicken rolls on the grate, cover grill and cook for about 10 minutes. Brush chicken rolls lightly with melted butter. Turn over, baste tops with additional butter and cook for 5 to 10 minutes longer or until meat is no longer pink, juices run clear and internal temperature reaches 165° to 170°. Remove toothpicks before serving chicken with warmed salsa.

For more kick, sprinkle 1 tablespoon diced green chile peppers on top of cheese before rolling chicken pieces.

For added flavor: 1) marinate chicken breasts before stuffing them; 2) baste stuffed chicken with a sauce during grilling; 3) drizzle a sauce on top of the grilled stuffed chicken just before serving.

BACON-VEGGIE-RANCH STUFFING

Fills 4 chicken breast halves

1 T. olive oil
4 tsp. brown sugar
½ C. diced red bell pepper
½ C. diced sweet onion
½ C. diced celery
8 slices bacon, cooked and crumbled
½ C. ranch-style salad dressing
4 slices mozzarella or provolone cheese
½ tsp. paprika
Seasoned salt to taste
Pinch of ground ginger to taste

Butterfly chicken breast halves as directed on page 14. Lightly brush the inside of each chicken breast with oil and sprinkle with brown sugar. In a small bowl, mix together bell pepper, onion and celery. Distribute vegetable mixture and crumbled bacon evenly over each piece. Roll chicken around the filling and secure with toothpicks. Brush with ranch dressing, cover and refrigerate for 1 hour.

To cook, lightly oil the grate and preheat grill to medium heat. Sprinkle each chicken roll with paprika, seasoned salt and ginger. Place chicken on the grate over heat, cover grill and cook for 7 to 10 minutes. Turn over and cover tops with mozzarella cheese. Cover grill and cook 7 to 10 minutes longer or until meat is no longer pink, juices run clear and internal temperature reaches 165° to 170°. Remove toothpicks before serving.

SESAME CHICKEN SALAD

Makes 8 servings

1½ C. light mayonnaise
2 T. sesame oil
2 T. sugar
¼ tsp. ground ginger
1 small head napa cabbage
4 grilled chicken breast halves prepared
    with Sesame Marinade (below) or Oriental
    Marinade (page 17)
8 green onions, chopped, divided
2 T. sesame seeds, toasted*
2 carrots, peeled and shredded
1 (20 oz.) can pineapple chunks,
    drained, optional
1 C. chow mein noodles

Several hours before serving, prepare the dressing by mixing together mayonnaise, oil, sugar and ginger. Cover and refrigerate. Slice the cabbage and place into a large bowl. Cut grilled chicken breast halves into strips or cubes and add to the bowl with cabbage. Add half of the green onions, sesame seeds, shredded carrot and optional pineapple chunks; toss lightly. To serve, drizzle dressing over salad and mix gently until coated. Top with noodles and remaining green onions.

Sesame Marinade: *Combine ¼ cup soy sauce, ¼ cup sesame oil, 1 tablespoon grated lemon peel, 2 tablespoons lemon juice, ½ teaspoon minced garlic and 1 to 2 teaspoons dried tarragon; mix well. Marinate chicken in the refrigerator for 12 to 18 hours before grilling. Discard marinade.*

* To toast, place sesame seeds in a small dry skillet over low heat and cook, stirring constantly, for 2 minutes or until golden and fragrant.

CHICKEN TENDERS

Chicken tenders can be cut from boneless skinless chicken breast halves. Simply slice the breasts into strips, 1" to 1½" wide and about 3" long. They cook quickly on the grill.

GRILLED CHICKEN TENDERS

Makes 6 servings

1½ lbs. chicken tenders (or boneless skinless chicken breast cut into strips)
½ C. buttermilk*
Salt and black pepper to taste

Wash chicken tenders and pat dry. In a large resealable plastic bag, combine chicken tenders and buttermilk. Seal bag and turn several times until chicken is well coated. Refrigerate to marinate tenders for 1 hour.

To cook, lightly oil the grate and preheat grill to medium-high heat. Remove chicken from bag, drain and pat dry. Discard marinade. Season chicken tenders with salt and pepper. Arrange chicken on the grate over heat and cook for 5 to 6 minutes, turning once partway through cooking. Remove from grill when meat is no longer pink, juices run clear and internal temperature reaches 165° to 170°.

* If buttermilk is not available, combine 1½ teaspoons vinegar or lemon juice with enough milk to make ½ cup. Stir and let mixture stand for 5 minutes before using like buttermilk.

SIMPLE FAJITA MARINADE

Marinates 1 lb. chicken tenders

¼ C. lime juice
1 T. vegetable oil
1 tsp. chili powder
¼ tsp. garlic powder, optional
Salt and black pepper to taste

In a small bowl, whisk together lime juice, oil, chili powder and garlic powder. Pour mixture over chicken tenders and refrigerate to marinate meat for 1 to 4 hours. To cook, remove chicken and discard marinade. Season chicken with salt and black pepper. Place tenders on lightly oiled grate and grill as directed above.

This marinade can also be used with beef steak to make beef fajitas.

CAESAR MARINADE

Marinates 1 to 1½ lbs. chicken tenders
½ C. creamy Caesar salad dressing
1 T. olive oil
Dash garlic powder
½ tsp. dried basil
1 tsp. dried minced onion
Dash black pepper

In a small bowl, whisk together dressing, oil, garlic powder, basil, onion and black pepper until blended. Pour mixture over chicken tenders and refrigerate to marinate meat for 1 to 2 hours. To cook, remove chicken and discard marinade. Place tenders on lightly oiled grate and grill as directed on page 21.

HONEY MUSTARD SAUCE

Makes about ¾ cup
⅓ C. mayonnaise
⅓ C. Dijon mustard
3 T. honey

In a small bowl, combine mayonnaise, Dijon mustard and honey; mix well. Serve as a dipping sauce with grilled chicken tenders.

HONEY MARMALADE SAUCE

Makes about 1 cup
½ C. honey
½ C. orange marmalade

Combine honey and marmalade in a small microwave-safe bowl. Cover and cook on high for 1 minute. Stir to blend and serve warm with grilled chicken tenders.

BETTER-THAN-KETCHUP SAUCE

Makes about ¾ cup
¾ C. ketchup
2 T. honey
1 T. Worcestershire sauce
2 drops hot sauce (or to taste)

In a small bowl, combine ketchup, honey, Worcestershire sauce and hot sauce; mix well. Serve as a dipping sauce with grilled chicken tenders.

Serve grilled chicken tenders with one of these delicious dipping sauces.

TROPICAL DIPPING SAUCE

Makes about 2 cups

1 C. honey mustard
1 C. pineapple preserves
½ tsp. curry powder

In a small bowl, combine honey mustard, preserves and curry powder; mix well and let stand for 30 minutes to combine flavors. Serve with grilled chicken tenders.

RANCH DIPPING SAUCE

Makes about 1 cup

⅓ C. buttermilk
½ C. sour cream
2 T. mayonnaise
1½ tsp. lemon juice
1 clove garlic, minced
¼ tsp. salt
⅛ tsp. black pepper
1 T. hot pepper sauce, optional

In a food processor or blender, combine buttermilk, sour cream, mayonnaise, lemon juice, garlic, salt, black pepper and optional pepper sauce; cover and process or blend until smooth. Chill and serve with grilled chicken tenders.

CREAMY GARLIC SAUCE

Makes about ½ cup

½ C. mayonnaise
2 tsp. red wine vinegar
1 tsp. garlic powder
½ tsp. dried basil
Salt and black pepper to taste

In a small bowl, whisk together mayonnaise, vinegar, garlic powder and basil. Season with salt and black pepper. Serve with grilled chicken tenders.

This sauce also tastes good with seafood.

CILANTRO PESTO

Garnishes 4 to 6 servings of chicken tenders

2 C. fresh cilantro leaves (1 to 2 bunches)
2 green onions or scallions, sliced
2 T. toasted sesame seeds*
1 T. lime juice
1 T. soy sauce
¾ tsp. vegetable oil
¼ tsp. chili powder

In a food processor or blender container, combine cilantro, onions, sesame seeds, lime juice, soy sauce, oil and chili powder. Process until almost smooth. Serve with grilled chicken tenders.

* To toast, place sesame seeds in a small dry skillet over low heat and cook, stirring constantly, for about 2 minutes or until golden and fragrant.

KIWIFRUIT SALSA

Garnishes 4 to 6 servings of chicken tenders

1½ C. peeled, diced kiwifruit (3 or 4)
1 orange, peeled and diced
1 C. peeled, diced jicama or apple
½ C. diced sweet red or yellow bell pepper
¼ C. chopped fresh cilantro
1 T. lime juice
1 T. vegetable oil
½ small jalapeño pepper, seeded and
   minced (or more to taste)
¼ tsp. salt

In a large bowl, combine kiwifruit, orange, jicama, bell pepper, cilantro, lime juice, oil, jalapeño pepper and salt; mix well. Chill for 30 minutes before serving with grilled chicken tenders.

CHIPOTLE CHICKEN FAJITAS

Makes 5 servings

1 (12 oz.) bottle chili sauce
¼ C. lime juice
4 chipotle peppers in adobo sauce (or to taste)
1 lb. chicken tenders, sliced into thin strips
½ C. cider vinegar
⅓ C. brown sugar
⅓ C. molasses
4 green bell peppers, cut into 1" pieces
1 onion, cut into 1" pieces
1 T. olive oil
⅛ tsp. salt
⅛ tsp. black pepper
10 (8") flour tortillas
1½ C. chopped tomatoes
1 C. shredded Mexican cheese blend

In a food processor, combine chili sauce, lime juice and chipotle peppers; cover and process until blended. Transfer ½ cup of mixture to a large resealable plastic bag. Add chicken tenders, seal bag and turn to coat well. Refrigerate bag to marinate chicken for 1 to 4 hours. Pour remaining marinade into a small bowl. Add vinegar, brown sugar and molasses; mix well. Cover and refrigerate.

To cook, lightly oil the grate and preheat grill to medium heat. On six metal or soaked wooden skewers, alternately thread pieces of chicken, green pepper and onion. Brush with oil and sprinkle with salt and black pepper. Place on the grate and cover grill; cook for 10 to 16 minutes, turning occasionally, or until chicken is no longer pink inside and juices run clear. Remove chicken and vegetables from skewers and place in a large bowl. Add ½ cup chipotle-molasses mixture and toss to coat; keep warm. Grill tortillas, uncovered, over medium heat for 45 to 55 seconds on each side or until warmed. Top each tortilla with a portion of the chicken mixture, tomatoes, cheese and remaining chipotle-molasses mixture; roll up and serve.

Turn grilled chicken tenders and flour tortillas into a spicy Mexican main dish that's sure to please.

CHICKEN WINGS

Grill wings over medium heat and turn frequently for even cooking. It will take 15 to 30 minutes to cook them thoroughly, depending on the size and thickness of wings.

GRILLED CHICKEN WINGS

Makes 8 to 10 servings
4 lbs. chicken wings (20 to 24 wings)
3 T. olive oil
2 tsp. salt
Bottled sauce of choice (like barbeque or hot sauce)

Rinse chicken wings and pat dry. Separate each wing at the joint to make two pieces. Cut off and discard wing tips.*

Lightly oil the grate and preheat grill to medium heat. Place remaining wing sections in a large bowl and drizzle with olive oil. Sprinkle with salt and work chicken pieces with hands until evenly coated.

To cook, arrange wings on the grate, cover grill and cook for 20 to 30 minutes or until tender and cooked through, turning occasionally. Juices should run clear and internal temperature in the thickest part should reach 165° to 180°. Remove from the grill and serve with sauce on the side for dipping, or coat grilled wings in the sauce before serving with additional dip. Use the instructions on the following pages for other spicy versions of hot wings.

* Trimmed wing tips may be frozen for future use in soups or casseroles.

TRADITIONAL BUFFALO SAUCE

Makes about ¾ cup
¼ C. melted butter
½ C. hot sauce

Prepare Grilled Chicken Wings as directed above. In a large bowl, combine melted butter and hot sauce. Add grilled wings to the bowl and toss until well coated. Serve hot with Blue Cheese Dip (recipe on page 28).

ZINGY HOT SAUCE

Makes about 1¾ cups
¼ tsp. cayenne pepper (or to taste)
¼ tsp. black pepper
1 T. soy sauce
1 C. Louisiana-style hot sauce (or to taste)
1 (12 oz.) can carbonated cola

Preheat the grill to medium heat. Rinse and cut up 4 pounds of chicken wings as directed on page 26. In a large pot, combine hot sauce, cola, cayenne pepper, black pepper and soy sauce; mix well. Place uncooked wings in the sauce and set pot on one side of the grill over indirect heat; cook until sauce is simmering. With tongs, remove wings from sauce and place them on lightly oiled grate over indirect heat for 8 to 10 minutes, turning once. Then return wings to the sauce to simmer for 5 to 10 minutes. Repeat this process for 50 minutes or until chicken is tender and pulls easily off the bone. The sauce will thicken as it cooks. If desired, return wings to the sauce one last time, or serve them right off the grill for drier wings.

ALL-PURPOSE CHICKEN RUB

Makes about ½ cup
3 T. Hungarian paprika*
1 T. black pepper
1 T. celery salt
1 to 2 T. sugar
1½ tsp. onion powder
1½ tsp. dry mustard
½ tsp. cayenne pepper
1½ tsp. finely grated lemon peel

In a small bowl, combine paprika, black pepper, celery salt, sugar, onion powder, dry mustard, cayenne pepper and lemon peel; mix well. Refrigerate in an airtight container for up to 5 months. To use, sprinkle mixture on trimmed, uncooked chicken wings and pat mixture evenly over skins. Grill as directed on page 26.

* Hungarian paprika is rich and sweet.

CREOLE RUB

Makes about ¾ cup

2½ T. paprika
2 T. salt
2 T. garlic powder
1 T. black pepper
1 T. onion powder
1 T. cayenne pepper
1 T. dried oregano
1 T. dried thyme

In a small bowl, combine paprika, salt, garlic powder, black pepper, onion powder, cayenne pepper, oregano and thyme; mix well. Store in an airtight container for up to 3 months. To use, sprinkle mixture on trimmed, uncooked chicken wings and pat mixture evenly over skin. Grill as directed on page 26.

BLUE CHEESE DIP

Makes about 2¾ cups

¾ C. sour cream
¾ C. mayonnaise
1 C. crumbled blue cheese
2 green onions, finely chopped
2 T. cider vinegar
1 T. Worcestershire sauce
¼ tsp. salt
Chilled celery and carrot sticks, optional

In a medium bowl, whisk together sour cream and mayonnaise. Add blue cheese, onion, vinegar, Worcestershire sauce and salt, stirring until well combined. Cover and refrigerate for several hours. Serve chilled dip with crisp vegetable sticks and any combination of the grilled chicken wings and sauces from pages 26–28.

PLUM DIP

Makes 1¼ cups

1 C. plum preserves
¼ C. golden raisins, chopped
2 T. minced onion
1 clove garlic, minced
1 T. white wine vinegar
2 tsp. prepared yellow mustard
2 tsp. prepared creamy horseradish
¼ tsp. salt

In a small saucepan over medium heat, combine preserves, raisins, onion, garlic, vinegar, mustard, horseradish and salt; mix well and cook until heated through, stirring frequently. Serve warm as a dipping sauce with Grilled Chicken Wings on page 26.

COCONUT CHICKEN WINGS

Makes 6 to 8 servings

3 lbs. chicken wings (15 to 18 wings)
3 T. olive oil
2 T. soy sauce
2 T. sugar
1 tsp. curry powder
½ tsp. salt
¼ tsp. black pepper
½ tsp. grated lemon peel
1 C. coconut milk
1 C. sweetened flaked coconut

Rinse chicken wings and separate each wing at the joint to make two pieces. Cut off and discard wing tips or freeze for another use. In a large bowl, whisk together oil, soy sauce, sugar, curry powder, salt, black pepper and lemon peel. Add coconut milk and whisk until blended. Reserve ½ cup of the mixture and divide it evenly between two small containers; refrigerate for basting and serving later. To remaining mixture, add chicken wings; toss until well coated. Cover and refrigerate to marinate wings for at least 1 hour or overnight.

Before grilling, heat a medium skillet over medium heat. Add coconut and toast for about 10 minutes or until golden brown, stirring constantly. Transfer toasted coconut to a plate to cool. Lightly crumble the flakes with fingers and set aside.

To cook, lightly oil the grates and preheat grill to medium heat. Remove wings from bowl and discard marinade. Arrange wings on the grate, baste with one container of reserved marinade and grill the wings for 8 to 10 minutes. Turn, baste again and cook for 8 to 10 minutes more or until meat is no longer pink. As wings finish cooking, transfer remaining reserved marinade to a small saucepan and heat thoroughly. Transfer the cooked wings to a platter and coat them with the warmed marinade. Sprinkle wings with toasted coconut and serve immediately.

Experience grilled chicken wings a whole new way with this recipe!

QUARTERS/PIECES

Save money by purchasing a whole fryer and cutting it up yourself, or choose your favorite pieces pre-packaged.

FAMILY-PLEASING GRILLED CHICKEN

Makes 8 servings

1 tsp. salt
1 tsp. black pepper
¾ tsp. brown sugar
¾ tsp. garlic powder
¾ tsp. onion powder
1 (3½ to 4 lb.) whole chicken, cut up*

Lightly oil the grate and preheat grill to medium heat. In a small bowl, combine salt, black pepper, brown sugar, garlic powder and onion powder; mix well. Sprinkle mixture over chicken pieces and pat evenly over skin.

To cook, place chicken on the grate over indirect heat, skin side up. Cover grill and cook for 15 to 20 minutes. Turn chicken, cover grill and cook for 20 to 40 minutes longer, turning occasionally, or until juices run clear and internal temperature reaches 165° to 170° for breasts and 165° to180° for thighs and legs.

* Choose legs, thighs, breasts, wings or quarters, adjusting cooking times for the size and type of pieces being grilled. The white meat of chicken breasts cooks more quickly than the dark meat of quarters, legs or thighs.

HONEY-MARGARITA MARINADE

Marinates 6 chicken quarters (or 12 individual pieces)

½ C. tequila
½ C. olive or sunflower oil
½ C. honey
¼ C. lime juice
1 tsp. finely grated lime peel
1 tsp. salt
2 cloves garlic, minced

In a medium bowl, whisk together tequila and oil until blended. Add honey, lime juice, lime peel, salt and garlic; mix well. Pour mixture over chicken and refrigerate to marinate pieces for 4 to 8 hours, turning occasionally. To cook, drain and discard marinade. Grill as directed.

This marinade may be covered and refrigerated for up to 2 days before use.

LEMON-OREGANO MARINADE

**Marinates 4 chicken quarters
(or 8 individual pieces)**

2 T. lemon juice
2 cloves garlic, minced
1 T. olive oil
1½ tsp. salt
1 tsp. finely grated lemon peel
2 T. chopped fresh oregano
Black pepper to taste

In a small bowl, whisk together lemon juice, garlic, oil, salt and lemon peel. Stir in oregano and black pepper. Pour marinade over chicken and refrigerate to marinate pieces for at least 1 hour or overnight, turning several times. To cook, drain and discard marinade. Grill as directed on page 30, turning frequently until golden brown on all sides.

Grill as directed on page 30

SOUTHWEST BEAN & CORN RELISH

**Garnishes 8 chicken quarters
(or 16 individual pieces)**

1 (11 oz.) can whole kernel white or yellow
  corn, drained
1 (15 oz.) can black beans, drained
  and rinsed
⅔ C. chopped red onion
¼ C. chopped fresh cilantro
3 T. lime juice
1 T. olive oil
1 clove garlic, minced
1 medium avocado, pitted, peeled and
  diced, optional

In a medium bowl, combine corn, beans, onion, cilantro, lime juice, oil, garlic and optional avocado; mix gently until combined. Cover and refrigerate for at least 1 hour to blend flavors. Spoon some of the relish on each serving plate and top with grilled chicken.

SPICY NECTARINE RELISH

**Garnishes 4 chicken quarters
(or 8 individual pieces)**

½ C. fresh raspberries
2 to 3 nectarines, peeled and cubed
1 T. minced jalapeño pepper (or more
  to taste)
½ C. sliced green onion
½ red bell pepper, diced
1 T. balsamic vinegar
1 tsp. maple syrup

In a medium bowl, combine raspberries, nectarines, jalapeño pepper, onion, bell pepper, vinegar and syrup; mix gently until well blended. Chill for several hours before serving alongside grilled chicken.

This relish also tastes good with other grilled meats.

TEXAS-STYLE BARBEQUE SAUCE

Makes about 2 cups

1 T. butter
1 clove garlic, minced
1 C. ketchup
⅓ C. brown sugar
⅓ C. Worcestershire sauce
¼ C. lemon juice
1 chipotle chile in adobo sauce, minced
  with seeds
¼ tsp. cayenne pepper
Salt and black pepper to taste

In a medium saucepan over medium heat, melt butter. Add garlic and sauté for 30 seconds. Stir in ketchup, brown sugar, Worcestershire sauce, lemon juice, chile and cayenne pepper. Bring mixture to a boil, reduce heat and simmer for 15 minutes, stirring occasionally, or until mixture is reduced to 1⅓ cups. Season with salt and black pepper. Cool slightly, cover and chill until needed. Sauce may be brushed on Family-Pleasing Grilled Chicken (page 30) during the last 15 minutes of grilling, or it may be served warm on the side.

This sauce also tastes good with grilled chicken tenders.

SOY-DIJON BASTING SAUCE

Makes about ¼ cup

2 T. soy sauce
1 T. olive oil
1 tsp. Dijon mustard
¼ tsp. salt
⅛ tsp. cayenne pepper
2 cloves garlic, minced

In a small bowl, combine soy sauce, oil, Dijon mustard, salt, cayenne pepper and garlic; mix well. Brush mixture over both sides of chicken pieces and then grill as directed on page 30.

PEANUT SAUCE

Makes about 2½ cups

1 tsp. vegetable oil
¼ C. chopped onion
1 clove garlic, minced
½ C. creamy peanut butter
4 tsp. soy sauce
1 tsp. brown sugar
⅛ tsp. ground ginger
⅛ tsp. cayenne pepper

In a small skillet over medium heat, heat oil. Add onion and garlic; sauté until tender. In a food processor or blender, combine sautéed vegetables, peanut butter, soy sauce, sugar, ginger and cayenne pepper; process until very smooth, adding ½ cup to 1 cup water to make a medium-thick consistency. Brush sauce over chicken pieces during the last 10 minutes of grilling Family-Pleasing Grilled Chicken on page 30. If desired, heat the sauce for several minutes and serve it on the side for dipping.

This sauce also tastes good with grilled chicken tenders or Thai Turkey Burgers (page 38).

TART CHERRY SAUCE

Makes about 2 cups
1¾ C. chicken broth
1 (12 oz.) jar tart cherry preserves
2 T. white wine vinegar
1 T. chopped fresh thyme leaves
   (or 1 tsp. dried thyme)
1 T. butter

In a medium saucepan over medium-high heat, bring chicken broth to a boil. Whisk in preserves, vinegar and thyme until preserves are melted; boil mixture for 8 minutes until slightly thickened. Whisk in butter until melted. Just before serving, drizzle sauce over Family-Pleasing Grilled Chicken on page 30.

This sauce also tastes good with grilled pork.

TASTY CHILI RUB

Makes about 1 tablespoon
1½ tsp. chili powder
1½ tsp. ground cumin
½ tsp. salt
⅛ tsp. black pepper

In a small bowl, combine chili powder, cumin, salt and black pepper; mix well. Sprinkle over chicken pieces and rub in with fingers before grilling as directed on page 30.

This is also a good rub for chicken breast halves and chicken tenders.

TROPICAL POULTRY RUB

Makes about ½ cup
2 T. ground ginger
2 T. brown sugar
2 T. finely grated orange peel
1 T. black pepper
1 T. salt
¼ tsp. ground nutmeg
¼ tsp. ground cloves

In a small bowl, combine ginger, brown sugar, orange peel, black pepper, salt, nutmeg and cloves; stir well. Sprinkle mixture on chicken and rub in with fingers, before grilling as directed on page 30. Mixture may be stored in an airtight container for several weeks.

This recipe should be doubled for use on a whole turkey.

BEER-BRINED GRILLED CHICKEN

Makes 4 servings

2 T. coarse salt
2 T. brown sugar
2 (12 oz.) cans regular or non-alcoholic
   beer, chilled
1 (3 to 3½ lb.) whole fryer chicken, quartered
1½ tsp. paprika
½ tsp. salt
¼ tsp. onion powder
¼ tsp. garlic powder
¼ tsp. black pepper
2 T. vegetable oil

In a 6- to 8-quart non-corrosive container (stainless steel, enamel-coated or plastic), combine 1 cup water with coarse salt and brown sugar, stirring until salt and sugar dissolve. Stir in beer. Add chicken, cover and refrigerate for 8 to 24 hours.

One hour before cooking, line a 9 x 13" baking pan with aluminum foil. Remove chicken from beer brine and discard brine. Rinse chicken with cool water and pat dry. Place chicken in pan and refrigerate uncovered for 1 hour to dry chicken skin. Meanwhile, in a small bowl, combine paprika, salt, onion powder, garlic powder and black pepper; mix well and set aside.

To cook, lightly oil the grate and preheat grill to medium heat, preparing it for indirect cooking. Brush oil over chicken and sprinkle with paprika mixture. Place chicken on the grate above the unheated side or over indirect heat and drip pan. Cover grill and cook for 15 minutes. Turn chicken, cover grill and cook for 20 to 30 minutes longer, turning occasionally, until juices run clear and internal temperature reaches 165° to 170° in the breast meat and 165° to 180° in the thigh.

PLANK-GRILLED CHICKEN

Makes 4 servings

2 (6 x 14 x ¾") oak or hickory grilling planks
1 (3 to 3½ lb.) whole fryer chicken, quartered
1 to 2 T. hot pepper sauce
1 to 2 tsp. coarsely cracked black pepper*
1 tsp. salt

At least 1 hour before grilling, soak grilling planks in water, placing a heavy dish on top to keep planks submerged. Loosen the skin on chicken pieces. In a small bowl, combine hot pepper sauce, black pepper and salt. Drizzle

mixture under the skin of chicken and rub to disperse mixture.

To cook on a charcoal grill, preheat briquettes to medium heat. Place planks on the rack directly over the coals until planks begin to crackle and smoke. Arrange chicken on planks, bone side down. Cover grill and cook for 15 to 20 minutes. Turn chicken and cook for 35 to 40 minutes longer or until juices run clear and internal temperature in thigh reaches 165° to 180°. For a gas grill, preheat grill to medium heat and grill as directed.

* To coarsely crack whole peppercorns, place them between two clean kitchen towels and roll over them with a rolling pin, or lightly hit with the flat side of a meat mallet.

WHOLE CHICKEN

A whole chicken (or turkey) can be grilled successfully if done slowly over indirect heat with a drip pan placed underneath the cooking area.

GRILLED CHICKEN ON A CAN

Makes 6 servings

1 T. paprika
2 tsp. salt
½ tsp. garlic powder
½ tsp. onion powder
½ tsp. black pepper
1 (4 to 4½ lb.) whole chicken
1 (12 oz.) can regular or non-alcoholic beer

For best results, use a charcoal grill with a drip pan placed directly under the grilling area. Add a small amount of water to pan. Arrange hot coals around the edge of the drip pan. If using a gas grill, use medium indirect heat.

In a small bowl, mix paprika, salt, garlic powder, onion powder and black pepper. Rinse chicken and pat dry. Fold wings of chicken across back with tips touching. Sprinkle paprika mixture inside chicken cavity and over outside of chicken; rub with fingers. Remove ½ cup of beer from the can. Holding chicken upright, with opening of body cavity down, insert beer can into cavity so chicken sits over can.

To cook, place chicken and can upright on the grate over the drip pan (or over unheated side of gas grill). Cover grill and cook for 1¼ to 1½ hours or until juices run clear, and the internal temperature of thigh meat reaches 165° to 180°. Using tongs and a large sturdy spatula under the can, carefully lift chicken and can off the grate and place it in a 9 x 13" pan. Let stand for 15 minutes before removing can and carving chicken. Discard can.

GINGER PEACH-GLAZED CHICKEN

Makes 6 servings

1 (4 to 5 lb.) whole chicken
Salt and black pepper to taste
½ C. peach preserves, large pieces chopped
1 T. white wine vinegar
1 T. prepared horseradish
1 tsp. freshly grated ginger
½ tsp. salt
½ tsp. coarsely ground black pepper

For best results use a charcoal grill with a drip pan placed directly under the grilling area. Add a small amount of water to the drip pan and arrange hot coals around the edge of the pan. If using a gas grill, use medium indirect heat.

Rinse chicken and pat dry. Pull the neck skin to the back and fasten with a short skewer. Tie drumsticks to tail with string. Fold wings of chicken across back with tips touching. Season with salt and pepper inside chicken cavity and over outside of chicken; rub with fingers.

To cook, place chicken on the grate over indirect heat, breast side up. Cover grill and cook for 1 hour. Cut string between drumsticks, cover and cook for 45 to 60 minutes more or until juices run clear and internal temperature of thigh meat reaches 165° to 180°.

Near the end of the cooking time, prepare glaze. In a small microwave-safe bowl, combine peach preserves, vinegar, horseradish, ginger, salt and black pepper. Stir well and microwave on high power for 30 to 60 seconds or until preserves are melted, stirring once. Brush preserves mixture over chicken several times during the last 15 minutes of grilling. Transfer chicken to a serving platter, cover loosely with foil and let stand 15 minutes before carving.

GROUND CHICKEN OR TURKEY

Ground chicken and ground turkey can be used inter-changeably in recipes. If you choose to grind only the white breast meat, rather than a traditional mix of white and dark meat, add a little extra seasoning and liquid binder, such as an egg. This will add flavor and moisture to the white meat, which tends to be drier and blander.

GRILLED CHICKEN BURGERS

Makes 4 servings

- 1 lb. uncooked ground chicken
- ½ C. finely chopped onion
- 2 tsp. dried basil, crushed (or other herb of choice)
- ½ tsp. seasoned salt
- ¼ tsp. black pepper
- ¼ tsp. hot pepper sauce, optional
- 4 hamburger buns or kaiser rolls, split
- **Condiments:** ketchup, barbeque sauce, mustard, pickles and onion slices

Lightly oil the grate and preheat grill to medium heat. In a medium bowl, combine ground chicken, onion, basil, seasoned salt, black pepper and hot pepper sauce; mix well, using hands as needed. Shape mixture into four patties, about ¾" thick. Place patties on the grate, cover grill and cook for 14 to 18 minutes, turning once, until internal temperature reaches 165°. Serve on buns with desired condiments.

CAJUN CHICKEN BURGERS

Makes 4 servings

- 1 lb. uncooked ground chicken
- ¼ C. garbanzo beans, drained and mashed
- 1 egg, lightly beaten
- 2 T. fine dry bread crumbs
- 1½ tsp. Cajun seasoning (purchased or use recipe below)
- ¼ tsp. salt
- 4 kaiser rolls or hamburger buns, split
- **Condiments:** lettuce leaves, tomato slices, chili sauce, ketchup

Lightly oil the grate and preheat grill to medium heat. In a large bowl, combine chicken, mashed beans, egg, bread crumbs, Cajun seasoning and salt; mix well, using hands as needed. Shape mixture into four patties, about ¾" thick. Place patties on the grate, cover grill and cook for 14 to 18 minutes, turning once, until internal temperature reaches 165°. Toast cut sides of rolls on grill. Serve on rolls with desired condiments.

Turn up the wild on 1 pound of plain uncooked ground chicken or turkey by adding these ingredients. Serve on buns or rolls as desired.

CAJUN SEASONING

Makes about ¼ cup

2 T. salt
1 T. cayenne pepper
1 tsp. ground white pepper
1 tsp. garlic powder
1 tsp. black pepper

In a small bowl, stir together salt, cayenne pepper, white pepper, garlic powder and black pepper. Store in an airtight container at room temperature.

Try this seasoning on pieces of chicken, too.

TACO CHICKEN BURGERS

Makes 4 servings

1 lb. uncooked ground chicken
½ small onion, diced
1 tsp. minced garlic
½ (1 oz.) pkg. dry taco seasoning mix
1 egg, lightly beaten
½ C. dry bread crumbs
Salt and black pepper to taste
Hamburger buns, split
Condiments: pepper-jack cheese, avocado slices, chopped jalapeño peppers, salsa

Lightly oil the grate and preheat grill to medium heat. In a large bowl, combine chicken, onion, garlic, taco seasoning, egg and bread crumbs; mix well, using hands as needed. Season with salt and black pepper. Shape mixture into four soft patties, about ½" thick. Place patties on the grate, cover grill and cook for 10 to 16 minutes, turning once, until internal temperature reaches 165°. Serve on buns topped with cheese, avocado, jalapeño peppers and salsa.

THAI TURKEY BURGERS

Makes 4 servings

1 egg, beaten
¼ C. fine dry bread crumbs
1 tsp. Thai seasoning or curry powder
1 lb. uncooked ground turkey breast
4 whole grain hamburger buns, split
¾ C. fresh basil leaves
2 T. peanut sauce (purchased or from recipe on page 32)
1 medium mango, pitted, peeled and sliced

Lightly oil the grate and preheat grill to medium heat. In a medium bowl, combine egg, bread crumbs and Thai seasoning. Add ground turkey and mix well. Shape into four soft patties, about ¾" thick. Place patties on the grate and cook for 14 to 18 minutes, turning once, until internal temperature reaches 165°. To serve, place a few basil leaves on the bottom half of each bun, add patties and spoon peanut sauce over patties. Top with mango slices and bun tops.

FRESH PEACHY-PEAR SALSA

Makes about 3 cups
⅓ C. purchased sweet and sour sauce
1 clove garlic, minced
2 tsp. chopped fresh cilantro
1 tsp. lemon juice
¼ tsp. crushed red pepper flakes
2 medium peaches, peeled, pitted
  and chopped
1 pear, cored and chopped
1 T. finely chopped red onion

In a medium bowl, combine sweet and sour sauce, garlic, cilantro, lemon juice and crushed red pepper; mix well. Stir in peaches, pear and onion until blended. Cover and chill salsa for up to 4 hours. Serve with chicken burgers.

MINTY CUCUMBER RELISH

Makes about 1¾ cups
1 C. chopped cucumber
½ C. chopped red onion
¼ C. chopped fresh mint
1 T. balsamic vinaigrette dressing
¼ tsp. salt

In a small bowl, combine cucumber, onion, mint, dressing and salt; mix well. Serve over chicken burgers.

Serve these tasty mixtures with Grilled Chicken (or turkey) Burgers.

TURKEY BREASTS

Large boneless, skinless turkey breasts can be cut into turkey steaks, tenders or cubes for a variety of tasty grilled entrees.

GRILLED TURKEY STEAKS

Makes 4 servings

4 (6 to 10 oz.) turkey breast fillets
(½" to ¾" thick)*
Salt and black pepper to taste

Lightly oil the grate and preheat grill to medium-high heat. Rub both sides of turkey pieces with salt and pepper to taste. Place turkey on the grate over direct heat and cook for 14 to 20 minutes, turning once, until no longer pink inside and internal temperature reaches 170°. Shorten grilling time for thinner cuts. Serve with relish or salsa.

* If not available at the grocery store, cut large whole turkey breasts or tenderloins into steaks by slicing horizontally. To make kebabs, turkey can be cut into strips (1" to 1½" wide) or 1" cubes to be threaded on skewers with chunks of vegetables or fruits before grilling. Cook kebabs over direct heat for approximately 10 to 15 minutes, turning frequently, until juices run clear and internal temperature reaches 165° to 170°.

CITRUS-GARLIC MARINADE

Marinates and bastes 4 turkey breast fillets

⅓ C. olive oil
¼ C. lemon juice
1 tsp. finely grated orange peel
¼ C. orange juice
¼ tsp. salt
¼ tsp. black pepper
4 cloves garlic, minced

In a small bowl, combine oil, lemon juice, orange peel, orange juice, salt, black pepper and garlic; mix well. Reserve ¼ cup of marinade for basting and refrigerate for later use. Pour remaining marinade over turkey steaks, strips or cubes and refrigerate to marinate turkey for 2 to 4 hours, turning occasionally.

To cook, lightly oil the grate and preheat grill to medium-high heat. Remove turkey and discard marinade. If making kebabs, thread turkey strips or cubes alternately with chunks of fresh vegetables or fruits on metal or soaked wooden skewers. Place turkey or skewers on the grate over medium heat, cover grill and cook for 10 to 15 minutes, turning once, until meat is no longer pink inside and internal temperature reaches 165° to 170°. Baste turkey with reserved marinade during the last half of grilling time.

SWEET APRICOT-PINEAPPLE GLAZE

Glazes 4 turkey breast fillets

2 T. butter
⅓ C. crushed pineapple with juice
½ C. apricot preserves

In a small saucepan over low heat, combine butter, pineapple and preserves; heat just until preserves melt, stirring well. Brush glaze over turkey during grilling as directed on page 40.

Use these recipes to marinate or baste turkey steaks before and during grilling. The recipes are also good with turkey strips and kebabs.

CRANBERRY-GRAPE RELISH

Garnishes 4 turkey breast fillets
½ C. fresh cranberries
½ C. blush wine or white grape juice
3 T. sugar
½ C. orange juice
1 lb. seedless green grapes, halved, divided
2 T. lime juice

In a medium saucepan over medium-low heat, combine cranberries, wine and sugar; bring mixture to a boil and cook until sugar dissolves. Add orange juice and half of the grapes, reduce heat to low and simmer mixture for 5 minutes. Remove from heat and add remaining grapes and lime juice; mix well and allow mixture to cool. Cover and refrigerate for up to 2 weeks. Serve relish on the side with grilled turkey.

CHERRY RELISH

Garnishes 4 turkey breast fillets
½ C. dried tart cherries
½ C. cherry preserves
2 T. red wine vinegar
½ C. chopped red onion
¼ yellow bell pepper, chopped
¼ green bell pepper, chopped
½ tsp. dried thyme

This relish also tastes good with grilled chicken and hamburgers.

In a medium microwave-safe bowl, combine cherries, preserves and vinegar; mix well and microwave on high power to 1 to 1½ minutes or until hot. Let mixture stand for 5 minutes. Stir in onion, both bell peppers and thyme; mix well. Cover and refrigerate for 3 hours or overnight. Serve with turkey.

ROASTED SWEET PEPPER & CITRUS SALSA

Garnishes 4 turkey breast fillets

 1 (7 oz.) jar roasted red sweet
  peppers, drained
 1 orange, peeled
 2 green onions, sliced
 2 T. balsamic vinegar
 1 T. snipped fresh basil

Chop the roasted peppers. Cut orange into small pieces, removing seeds. In a small bowl, combine chopped peppers, orange pieces, onions, vinegar and basil; mix well. Cover and chill. Serve with grilled turkey.

GREEK SALSA

Garnishes 4 turkey breast fillets

 2 T. white wine vinegar
 2 tsp. olive oil
 1 tsp. Greek seasoning
 1 C. finely chopped tomato
 ¼ C. finely chopped cucumber
 ¼ C. finely chopped, pitted kalamata
  or black olives
 ¼ C. chopped red onion
 Feta cheese, optional

In a medium bowl, combine vinegar, oil and Greek seasoning. Stir in tomato, cucumber, olives and onion until blended. Spoon salsa over grilled turkey or turkey burgers, and top with a sprinkling of feta cheese, if desired.

TURKEY DRUMSTICKS

Turkey drumsticks range in weight from ½ to 1½ pounds each. Grill them slowly to assure meat is fully cooked, tender and juicy. Marinades, seasonings and glazes add flavor.

GRILLED TURKEY DRUMSTICKS

Makes 4 servings

2 tsp. brown sugar
1 tsp. coarse salt
1 tsp. garlic powder
1 tsp. paprika
1 tsp. black pepper
¼ C. mayonnaise (or olive oil), divided
4 turkey drumsticks

Lightly oil the grate and preheat grill to medium indirect heat. In a small bowl, mix together brown sugar, salt, garlic powder, paprika and black pepper. Rinse drumsticks under cool water and pat dry with paper towels. Spread 1 tablespoon mayonnaise on each drumstick (or more) and then sprinkle evenly with seasoning mixture.

To cook, place drumsticks on the grate over indirect heat and cover grill. Grill slowly for 1 to 1¼ hours*, turning frequently, or until drumsticks are browned, tender and internal temperature reaches 165° to 180°. Baste occasionally during grilling with a sauce or glaze as desired.

* Adjust grilling time for the size of drumsticks used.

DRUMSTICK BARBEQUE SAUCE

Makes about 2¾ cups

1 T. butter
1 medium onion, finely chopped
½ C. chopped celery
1 (8 oz.) can tomato sauce
½ C. ketchup
2 T. brown sugar
1 to 2 T. prepared yellow mustard
1 T. Worcestershire sauce

In a large saucepan over medium heat, melt butter. Add onion and celery; sauté until tender. Add 1 cup water, tomato sauce, ketchup, brown sugar, mustard and Worcestershire sauce. Mix well and keep mixture warm over low heat. Grill drumsticks as directed above. When drumsticks are almost done, remove ½ cup of the sauce for basting. Baste the drumsticks, turn and continue to grill for 10 to 15 minutes longer or until fully cooked and internal temperature reaches 165° to 180°. Bring remaining sauce in saucepan to a boil and serve it on the side.

SWEET 'N' HOT DRUMSTICK SIMMERING SAUCE

Makes 6 turkey drumsticks

1 (2 liter) bottle lemon-lime soda
2 T. sugar
2 T. hot pepper sauce
1 T. crushed red pepper flakes
1 T. black pepper
1 large sweet onion, thickly sliced
2 T. honey
1 T. steak seasoning

In a large pot, stir together soda, sugar, hot pepper sauce, red pepper flakes, black pepper and onion. Add turkey legs and bring mixture to a boil. Reduce heat and simmer for 30 to 45 minutes or until turkey has reached an internal temperature of 165° to 180°.

To finish cooking drumsticks on the grill, lightly oil the grate and preheat grill to medium-high heat. Remove onion slices from mixture and arrange them on the grate. Place drumsticks over the onions. Drizzle with honey and sprinkle with steak seasoning. Cook for 20 minutes or until a crisp brown crust forms, turning once.

Use sauce to prepare and add flavor to grilled turkey drumsticks.

BEEF

BASIC COOKING TIPS

To ensure safety and quality, grilled beef must be cooked to the minimum internal temperatures listed below. Larger cuts, like roasts, benefit from 15 minutes of standing time before carving. Since color is not a reliable indicator of doneness in beef, it is best to use a meat thermometer to measure internal temperature.

Tender cuts of beef can be cooked by direct or indirect heat. Less tender cuts of meat require tenderizing and should be cooked with indirect heat for best results. Tenderizing can be done by pounding with a meat mallet, scoring with a sharp knife or marinating in a mixture containing an acidic ingredient like lemon juice, vinegar or wine. Meat should always be refrigerated during marinating.

	Cook to *this internal temperature*
Beef steaks & beef roasts	**145° to 170°**
rare/medium rare	**145°**
medium	**160°**
well-done	**170°**
Ground beef	**160°**

TENDER STEAKS

To grill steaks, trim excess fat from the outer edges and slit remaining fat at 2" intervals to prevent steaks from curling during cooking. Steaks are generally ¾" to 1½" thick and cooking time will depend on the heat, thickness of the cut and preferred degree of doneness.

GRILLED SIRLOIN STEAK

Makes 4 servings

2 (12 to 14 oz.) beef top sirloin steaks*
Salt and black pepper to taste
Seasoned salt or garlic salt, optional

Sprinkle steaks with salt, black pepper and other seasonings to taste. Lightly oil the grate and preheat grill to medium-high heat. Place steaks on grate over direct heat and grill for 14 to 22 minutes (if 1" thick), turning once halfway through cooking time. Adjust time for steak's thickness and the degree of doneness desired. To serve, cut each steak in half and top with a favorite sauce.

* Other tender beef steaks may be substituted such as or T-bone, porterhouse, ribeye, flat iron or tenderloin. Tenderloin steaks (also called filet mignon) are often wrapped with bacon to add flavor since they have very little fat of their own to flavor the meat.

SAVORY STEAK SAUCE

Makes about ½ cup

3 T. bottled A-1 steak sauce (Spicy or Original)
2 T. ketchup
2 T. orange marmalade
1 T. lemon juice
1 T. finely chopped onion
1 clove garlic, minced

In a small bowl, combine steak sauce, ketchup, marmalade, lemon juice, onion and garlic; mix well. Reserve ¼ cup of mixture for serving and use the rest for basting steak during grilling. Warm up reserved sauce mixture before serving with steak.

CHEESE STEAK SAUCE

Makes enough for 4 Philly-style steak sandwiches

2 T. butter
2 T. flour
2 C. whole milk
1½ to 2 C. shredded sharp Cheddar cheese
2 tsp. dry mustard
Salt and black pepper to taste
4 soft Italian rolls, split
Optional condiments: grilled onions, mushrooms, green bell pepper and hot chile peppers

In a medium saucepan over medium heat, melt butter. Whisk in flour and cook for 1 minute. Slowly whisk in the milk and cook until thickened. Whisk in the cheese, cooking until it melts. Add dry mustard and season with salt and pepper. Place thinly sliced beef steaks on Italian rolls and top with warmed cheese sauce.

To make Philly-Style Steak Sandwiches, add grilled onions, mushrooms, bell pepper and chile peppers.

ROSEMARY-GARLIC RUB

Seasons 4 steaks

2 T. chopped fresh rosemary
1½ tsp. seasoned salt
1 tsp. garlic pepper
½ tsp. garlic powder with parsley
1 T. olive oil

In a small bowl, combine rosemary, seasoned salt, garlic pepper and garlic powder with parsley; mix well. Before grilling, brush each steak with a little olive oil. Sprinkle with herb mixture, pressing it on evenly with fingers. Grill steaks to desired doneness as directed on page 47.

THREE PEPPER STEAK RUB

Seasons 4 steaks

2 tsp. black peppercorns
2 tsp. white peppercorns
2 tsp. Szechwan peppercorns
⅛ tsp. ground allspice

Place all peppercorns between two layers of waxed paper and crush them coarsely with a rolling pin. Mix crushed peppercorns with allspice. Rub mixture on both sides of steak, cover and refrigerate for 1 to 2 hours before grilling. Grill steaks to desired doneness as directed on page 47.

Try one of these rubs before grilling tender beef steaks.

SHISH KEBABS

To turn tender sirloin steak into shish kebabs, cut steak into 1" cubes and marinate before threading onto skewers with other foods and grilling. To make fajitas, simply cut steak into thin strips after grilling.

BASIC GRILLED SHISH KEBABS

Makes 4 servings

- ½ C. sweet and tangy steak sauce (such as Heinz 57)
- ¼ C. lime juice
- 1½ lbs. boneless beef sirloin steak, cut into 1" cubes
- Salt and black pepper to taste

Choice of fresh vegetables: red, green or yellow sweet bell peppers, cut in chunks; onions, cut in chunks; new potatoes, cut in half and parboiled for 10 to 12 minutes or until almost tender; cherry tomatoes; mushrooms; pineapple chunks.

In a small bowl, combine steak sauce and lime juice; mix well. Pour ½ cup of mixture into a large resealable plastic bag and add beef cubes. Seal bag and refrigerate to marinate meat for 1 hour, turning several times. Cover remaining marinade and refrigerate for basting later.

To cook, lightly oil the grate and preheat grill to medium heat. Remove meat from bag and discard marinade. On metal or soaked wooden skewers, alternately thread meat, potatoes and other vegetables as desired*. Sprinkle with salt and black pepper. Place kebabs on the grate and cook for 9 to 15 minutes or to desired doneness, turning often. Brush kebabs lightly with reserved sauce mixture during the last few minutes of cooking time.

* If preferred, make separate skewers of meat and similar vegetables to assure even grilling. Grill onion and bell pepper kebabs for 10 minutes; grill tomato and mushroom kebabs for 7 minutes.

TACO MARINADE

Marinates 1 to 1½ lbs. beef cubes

- 1 C. tomato juice
- 3 T. vegetable oil
- 1 (1.25 oz.) env. taco seasoning

In a small bowl, combine tomato juice, oil and taco seasoning; mix well. Pour ¾ cup of mixture into a large resealable plastic bag and add beef cubes. Seal bag and refrigerate for 1 hour, turning several times. Refrigerate remaining marinade for basting later. To cook, assemble and grill kebabs as directed above, using reserved marinade to baste kebabs near end of grilling time.

TERIYAKI MARINADE

Marinates 1 to 1½ lbs. beef cubes
½ C. ketchup
½ C. sugar
½ C. soy sauce
1 tsp. garlic powder
1 tsp. ground ginger

In a small bowl, combine ketchup, sugar, soy sauce, garlic powder and ginger; mix well. Pour 1 cup of mixture into a large resealable plastic bag and add beef cubes. Seal bag and refrigerate to marinate meat for 2 hours or overnight, turning several times. Refrigerate remaining marinade for basting later. To cook, assemble and grill kebabs as directed on page 49. Boil reserved marinade for at least 1 minute. Serve shish kebabs with warm marinade.

Other easy marinades to try: bottled ranch-style salad dressing, bottled Italian salad dressing, Fajita marinade made with an envelope of fajita seasoning mix.

INDIVIDUAL STEAK PIZZAS

Makes 8 servings
1 lb. boneless beef sirloin steak
2 tsp. steak seasoning, divided
1 onion
1 green, red or yellow bell pepper
1 T. plus 1 tsp. olive oil, divided
1 (13.8 oz.) tube refrigerated pizza dough
1 C. prepared pizza sauce
2 C. shredded mozzarella or Monterey Jack cheese, divided
8 oz. crumbled blue cheese, optional

Lightly oil the grate and preheat grill to medium heat. Sprinkle both sides of steak with seasoning. Place steak on the grate and cook for 5 to 7 minutes on one side. Meanwhile, cut the onion and bell pepper into thick slices and brush with 1 teaspoon oil. Arrange vegetables on the grate to cook. Turn steaks and cook for 5 to 7 minutes longer or to desired doneness while vegetables continue to cook until tender-crisp. Remove steak and vegetables from the grill and cut into bite-size pieces; set aside.

Unroll dough and cut into four equal pieces. On a floured board, pat out each piece to larger rectangles about ¼" thick; brush top of each piece with remaining tablespoon oil. Place dough on the grate, oiled side down. Close lid and cook for 1 to 2 minutes or until grill marks show on crusts. Use tongs or a large spatula to carefully flip each crust over on the grate, moving it to indirect heat. Spread a portion of the sauce on each crust. Sprinkle about half of the mozzarella cheese over the four pizzas. Top each pizza with grilled steak, vegetables and optional blue cheese. Sprinkle remaining mozzarella cheese on top. Close grill lid and cook pizzas for 3 to 4 minutes longer or until cheese is melted and crust is browned. Check pizzas often and rotate as needed for even baking. Slide pizzas onto a clean baking sheet before serving.

Try a new twist on steak by layering it with other ingredients on a grilled pizza!

LESS TENDER STEAKS

Some steaks are less tender but very flavorful and economical. Flank, round, shoulder, plate or skirt steaks should be marinated, scored or pounded before grilling. They can be served in whole pieces or sliced to use in salads, wraps, fajitas or on pizza.

GRILLED SKIRT STEAK

Makes 4 to 6 servings

1½ to 2 lbs. beef skirt steak*
Sea salt and black pepper to taste
2 tsp. onion powder
2 tsp. garlic powder
2 T. white wine vinegar
2 T. olive oil

Trim fat and cut steak into 4 to 6 even pieces. Rub a generous amount of salt and pepper into both sides of each steak. Pat some of the onion powder and garlic powder into each piece. Place steaks in a shallow glass dish and sprinkle vinegar over the tops; brush each piece with some of the oil. Cover and refrigerate to marinate meat at least 4 hours or up to 24 hours.

To cook, lightly oil the grate and preheat the grill to medium heat. Remove steaks from dish and place them on the grate; grill for 5 to 8 minutes, or to desired doneness, turning once halfway through cooking. Remove from the grill and let rest for 5 minutes before serving. If desired, slice the steaks thinly across the grain before serving. Drizzle with sauce or top with fruit salsa, if desired.

* You may substitute other less tender steaks, such as flank or round steak.

ALL-PURPOSE BEEF MARINADE

Marinates 2 lbs. steak

¾ C. vegetable oil
¼ C. soy sauce
1 T. lemon pepper
2 tsp. Worcestershire sauce
4 to 6 drops hot pepper sauce (or to taste)

In a large resealable plastic bag, combine oil, soy sauce, lemon pepper, Worcestershire sauce, hot pepper sauce and ⅔ cup water; mix well. Add steaks, seal bag and refrigerate to marinate meat for 4 hours or overnight. To cook, remove steak from bag and discard marinade. Grill meat as directed above.

SAUCY CAPER MARINADE

Marinates 1½ lbs. steak

¼ C. A-1 steak sauce (Original)
1 tsp. minced garlic
¼ C. capers

In a blender, combine steak sauce, garlic and capers; blend until smooth. Place steaks in a shallow glass dish and pour sauce over, turning steaks to coat both sides. Cover and refrigerate to marinate meat for at least 1 hour. To cook, remove steaks from dish and grill as directed on page 51.

CHINESE MARINADE & BASTING SAUCE

Marinates and bastes 1½ lbs. steak

2 T. hoisin sauce
2 T. orange juice
2 T. rice vinegar
2 T. soy sauce

In a large resealable plastic bag, combine hoisin sauce, orange juice, vinegar and soy sauce; mix well. Add steak to the bag, seal and turn bag to coat meat. Refrigerate to marinate steak at least 30 minutes. To cook, remove meat from bag and discard marinade. Grill steak as directed on page 51.

To make lettuce wraps, slice steak into thin strips before marinating. After grilling meat on a grill rack, serve with large lettuce leaves for wrapping.

CHIMICHURRI BASTING SAUCE

Bastes and garnishes 2 lbs. steak

½ C. olive oil
2 T. malt or red wine vinegar
3 T. dried minced parsley
2 T. minced onion
2 cloves garlic, minced
1 tsp. dried oregano
1 bay leaf
⅛ tsp. cayenne pepper
½ tsp. paprika
½ tsp. salt
¼ tsp. black pepper

In a small bowl, combine oil, vinegar, parsley, onion, garlic, oregano, bay leaf, cayenne pepper, paprika, salt and black pepper; mix well. Cover and let mixture stand at room temperature for 8 hours. To use, drizzle some sauce over both sides of scored beef and rub it in well. Grill meat as directed on page 51. Spoon some of the remaining sauce over cooked meat before serving.

WATERMELON & PEACH SALSA

Garnishes 4 to 6 servings

1½ C. chopped watermelon, seeds removed
½ C. peeled, chopped fresh peaches
¼ C. finely chopped jalapeño peppers, seeds removed
1 T. capers
¼ C. chopped fresh cilantro
¼ C. balsamic vinaigrette dressing

In a medium bowl, combine watermelon, peaches, jalapeño peppers, capers, cilantro and dressing; mix well. Top sliced steak with salsa before serving.

CHARRED TOMATO SALSA

Garnishes 4 to 6 servings

2 medium tomatoes, cored, halved and seeded
½ C. thinly sliced red onion
1 T. red wine vinegar
1 tsp. olive oil
¼ tsp. salt
⅛ tsp. black pepper
6 fresh basil leaves, chopped

Place tomato halves on paper towels, cut side down; let stand 30 minutes. Lightly oil a grill pan and preheat grill to medium-high heat. Arrange tomato halves on pan, cut sides down, and cook for 5 minutes. Turn tomatoes over and grill skin side for 1 minute or until skin is blackened. Remove from pan and cool 5 minutes. Cut tomatoes into 1" pieces and place in a medium bowl; add onion, vinegar, oil, salt, black pepper and basil; stir to blend. Top sliced steak with salsa before serving.

These recipes add color and flavor when used to garnish beef steaks.

BEEF ROASTS

Tender roasts can be grilled successfully, such as top sirloins, sirloin tri tips or rib roasts. Avoid grilling roasts that are less tender and need moist heat cooking methods, such as most chuck and round roasts. Roasts should be seared over direct heat to seal in juices and then cooked slowly over indirect heat to achieve an even level of doneness inside.

GRILLED ITALIAN BEEF ROAST

Makes 12 to 14 servings
1 (3 to 4 lb.) boneless beef sirloin tip roast
1 to 2 T. olive oil
1 (0.7 oz.) env. Italian dressing mix

Place grate 4" to 5" above heat. Lightly oil the grate and preheat grill for high heat for first part of grilling. Brush roast with oil and sprinkle dry Italian dressing evenly over meat; let stand at room temperature for about 15 minutes. Place roast on grate over direct heat and sear each side for 5 to 8 minutes or until well browned. Reduce heat and set up burners or charcoal for indirect grilling. Move the roast to the unheated part of grill for indirect heat. Cover grill and cook at about 300° for 1½ hours without opening lid. Then open lid and insert a grill-safe meat thermometer into the thickest part of the meat. Cover and continue to cook the roast until thermometer reaches 145° to 150°. Allow 30 to 90 minutes of additional time to cook roast to desired doneness. Remove roast from the grill and place it on a carving surface. Cover meat with foil and let stand 15 minutes to allow the internal temperature to rise about 5°. This will make the roast juicier and easier to carve.

RICH BEEF RUB

Makes about ½ cup
¼ C. salt
2 T. paprika
1 T. coarse black pepper
1½ tsp. onion powder
1½ tsp. garlic powder
1½ tsp. cayenne pepper
½ tsp. coriander
½ tsp. turmeric

In a small bowl, combine salt, paprika, black pepper, onion powder, garlic powder, cayenne pepper, coriander and turmeric; mix well. Store in an airtight container and sprinkle or rub on any cut of beef before grilling.

SALT-FREE BEEF RUB

Makes about ½ cup

2 T. sugar
1 tsp. garlic powder
1 tsp. cayenne pepper
¼ tsp. black pepper
½ tsp. white pepper
2 tsp. onion powder
1 tsp. paprika
2 tsp. filé powder
2 tsp. dried thyme
2½ tsp. dried basil
½ tsp. dried oregano

In a small bowl, combine sugar, garlic powder, cayenne pepper, black pepper, white pepper, onion powder, paprika, filé powder, thyme, basil and oregano; mix well. Store in an airtight container and sprinkle or rub on any cut of beef before grilling.

BOURBON STREET MARINADE

Makes about 3 cups

⅔ C. soy sauce
½ C. bourbon
3 T. Worcestershire sauce
2 T. lemon juice
¼ C. brown sugar

In a large resealable plastic bag, combine soy sauce, bourbon, Worcestershire sauce, lemon juice, brown sugar and 1½ cups water; mix well. Remove ⅓ cup of mixture to a small bowl; cover and refrigerate for basting. To the bag, add one (4 to 6 pound) beef roast, 1½" to 2" thick. Seal bag and turn to coat meat. Refrigerate 8 hours or overnight. To cook, remove roast and discard marinade. Grill as directed on page 54. Brush beef with reserved marinade and turn halfway through cooking time.

ZESTY BEEF SAUCE

Makes about 1¾ cups

1 (10¾ oz.) can tomato soup
2 T. brown sugar
2 T. lemon juice
2 T. vegetable oil
1 T. Worcestershire sauce
1 tsp. garlic powder
¼ tsp. crushed dried thyme leaves

In a medium bowl, whisk together soup, brown sugar, lemon juice, oil, Worcestershire sauce, garlic powder and thyme. Reserve ⅔ of the mixture and refrigerate until needed. Use remaining mixture to baste roast during the last half of grilling as directed on page 54. Before serving, boil reserved mixture for 3 minutes. Serve warm sauce with grilled sliced roast beef or other cuts of grilled beef.

BEEF RIBS

To grill ribs successfully, first marinate them overnight to increase tenderness; then sear all sides over hot direct heat before finishing by slow grilling over indirect heat. Ribs may also be parboiled before cooking on the grill. Use a grill with a tight cover.

SLOW-COOKED BEEF SHORT RIBS

Makes 5 servings

10 beef short ribs (each approximately 3" long)
Salt and black pepper to taste
Olive oil
1 qt. beef broth (or water)
1 onion, coarsely chopped
1 (1 oz.) env. dry onion soup mix
2 C. sliced fresh mushrooms, optional
4 medium potatoes, peeled and cut into bite-size chunks

Preheat grill to high heat. Rinse ribs and pat dry. Peel off membrane on the back side of ribs. Sprinkle salt and black pepper generously over ribs and drizzle with oil. Place ribs on grate directly over heat and sear all sides for 1 to 2 minutes. When browned, transfer ribs to a grill-safe 9 x 13" pan placed over indirect heat. Pour broth over the ribs in pan. Arrange chopped onions on top and sprinkle dry soup mix over the ribs. Spread sliced mushrooms and potato chunks on top. Cover the grill and cook ribs in the pan over indirect heat (approximately 225°) for 4 to 5 hours, basting the ribs with pan juices every 30 to 45 minutes. Ribs are done when cooked through and very tender. Baste ribs one last time before moving them to a serving plate*. Serve with the potatoes and some of the juice, mushrooms and onions over the top.

* Ribs may be finished on the grate over direct heat for a few minutes before serving, if desired. See page 13 for additional information about direct and indirect heat.

SWEET CHILI POWDER RUB

Makes about ½ cup
2 T. paprika
2 T. chili powder
2 T. brown sugar
2 T. black pepper
1½ tsp. cayenne pepper
1½ tsp. garlic powder
1½ tsp. salt

In a small bowl, mix together paprika, chili powder, brown sugar, black pepper, cayenne pepper, garlic powder and salt. To use, sprinkle over uncooked ribs and grill as directed on page 56. Mixture may be stored in an airtight container for later use.

LEMON PEPPER RUB

Makes about ¼ cup
3 T. sea salt
½ tsp. black pepper
1 tsp. garlic powder
1 tsp. lemon pepper
1 tsp. paprika

In a small bowl, mix together salt, black pepper, garlic powder, lemon pepper and paprika. To use, sprinkle over uncooked ribs and grill as directed on page 56. Mixture may be stored in an airtight container for later use.

This rub is good with grilled salmon and other seafood, as well as pork chops and chicken.

COLA MARINADE

Marinates 4 lbs. beef ribs
1 C. carbonated cola beverage
1½ C. soy sauce
2 T. rice wine vinegar
1 T. red pepper flakes
6 cloves garlic, mashed
1 small red onion, chopped

In a large resealable plastic bag, mix cola, soy sauce, vinegar, pepper flakes, garlic and onion. Add ribs, seal bag and refrigerate for 24 hours.

To cook, lightly oil the grate and preheat grill to medium heat. Discard marinade. Place ribs on the grate, cover grill and cook for 20 to 25 minutes or to desired doneness, turning once. (Ribs may also be cooked over indirect heat for about 1 hour.)

SWEET & SPICY RIB MARINADE

BEEF

Beef Ribs

Marinates 4 to 5 lbs. beef ribs

2 C. orange juice
½ C. balsamic vinegar
½ C. olive oil
½ C. Worcestershire sauce
1 T. soy sauce
1 tsp. hot pepper sauce
1 T. dry mustard
1 T. garlic powder
1 tsp. chili powder
1 tsp. paprika

In a large resealable plastic bag, mix orange juice, vinegar, oil, Worcestershire sauce, soy sauce, hot sauce, dry mustard, garlic powder, chili powder and paprika. Remove, reserve and refrigerate ⅓ of mixture. Add ribs to bag, seal and refrigerate for 4 to 6 hours.

To cook, oil the grate and preheat grill to medium-high indirect heat. Simmer reserved marinade. Discard soaking marinade; grill ribs for 1 hour, turning and basting frequently with part of reserved marinade. Transfer fully cooked ribs to a pan; baste again, cover and let stand 10 minutes before serving.

Make beef ribs extra-tasty when you use one of these seasoning rubs before grilling. Or for flavor and tenderness, marinate ribs before grilling.

GROUND BEEF

When making burgers, ground chuck is a good choice for flavor and just the right amount of fat to make juicy burgers that aren't greasy. Avoid pressing down on the burgers with a spatula while cooking, which squeezes out the juices.

BASIC GRILLED HAMBURGER

Makes 4 servings

1½ lbs. ground chuck (85% lean)
1 tsp. salt
1 tsp. freshly ground black pepper
4 slices American cheese, optional
Nonstick cooking spray or vegetable oil
4 hamburger buns, split and buttered
Condiments: ketchup*, mustard, mayonnaise, lettuce and pickle, onion, cucumber and tomato slices

Lightly oil the grate and preheat grill to medium-high. In a large bowl, combine ground chuck, salt and black pepper, mixing lightly with hands until well blended. Use a fork to shape mixture into four patties, about ¾" thick and ½" larger than the diameter of hamburger buns. Spray both sides of each beef patty with cooking spray (or brush lightly with vegetable oil). Place patties on the grate, close grill lid and cook for 3 to 4 minutes undisturbed. Flip patties once, add optional cheese, close the lid and continue to cook 3 to 4 additional minutes or until juices run clear and the internal temperature reaches 160° on a meat thermometer. Toast buttered side of buns briefly on the grill until golden brown and crunchy. Place one beef patty inside each bun and serve with condiments as desired.

* Chipotle Ketchup: *In a small bowl, whisk together 1 cup ketchup, 1 to 3 tablespoons pureed canned chipotle in adobo sauce, ¼ teaspoon salt and ¼ teaspoon black pepper. Cover and refrigerate for at least 30 minutes. Mixture can be refrigerated in an airtight container for up to 1 week and used in place of regular ketchup.*

Prepare and cook four Basic Grilled Hamburgers following the recipe above. Then go wild with any of the toppers and buns on page 60.

BEEF

Ground Beef

ZIPPY ONION BURGER TOPPER

Tops 4 burgers
1 T. olive oil
1 lb. sweet onions, thinly sliced and
    separated into rings
2 T. Miracle Whip salad dressing
1½ T. A-1 steak sauce (Original)
4 toasted hamburger buns

In a large nonstick skillet over medium-high heat, heat oil. Add onions and sauté for 10 minutes or until golden, stirring often. Add dressing and steak sauce, mixing well. Spoon some onion mixture on each grilled hamburger patty and serve on toasted buns.

PIZZA BURGER

Tops 4 burgers
¼ C. pizza sauce, warmed, divided
12 to 20 thin slices pepperoni, divided
½ C. shredded mozzarella cheese, divided
4 toasted hamburger buns

On each hot grilled hamburger patty, spread approximately 1 tablespoon pizza sauce; arrange 3 to 5 pepperoni slices and 2 tablespoons mozzarella cheese over sauce. Serve on toasted buns.

GOURMET BISTRO BURGER

Makes 4 servings
3 T. vegetable oil
1 onion, sliced into half-rings
Salt and black pepper to taste
4 wheat or multi-grain buns
4 slices Brie cheese, room temp.
4 tsp. real bacon bits

In a large skillet over medium-low heat, combine oil and onions, stirring until well coated. Season with salt and black pepper. Cook onions, stirring occasionally, until tender, browned and reduced to half the original size. Grill burgers as directed on page 59. Serve on wheat or multi-grain buns topped with cooked onions, cheese and bacon bits.

GRILLED HERBED MUSHROOMS

Makes 4 servings

2 T. olive oil
1 T. butter
1½ C. chopped crimini or
   shiitake mushrooms
1 finely chopped green onion
Salt and black pepper to taste
1 T. chopped fresh thyme leaves
2 T. chopped fresh flat-leaf parsley leaves
4 onion buns, toasted
¼ C. crumbled blue cheese, optional

In a large skillet over high heat, combine oil and butter; heat until almost smoking. Add mushrooms and cook until soft, stirring occasionally, about 5 minutes. Add onion and season with salt and black pepper. Cook until mushrooms are golden brown, about 5 more minutes. Stir in thyme and parsley, and transfer to a bowl. Grill burgers as directed on page 59. Serve burgers on toasted onion buns topped with a spoonful of the mushroom mixture and blue cheese, if desired.

Try these grilled mushrooms on top of beef steaks, too.

ASIAN BURGER

Makes 4 servings

1 lb. ground chuck (or lean ground beef)
½ tsp. curry powder
½ tsp. cumin
½ tsp. sugar
1½ T. chopped cilantro
2 tsp. finely chopped green onion
1 minced Thai bird chile (or jalapeño or
   Serrano pepper)
Salt and black pepper to taste
6 green onions or scallions
4 shiitake mushroom caps
2 T. teriyaki sauce
4 sesame hamburger buns

Lightly oil the grate and preheat grill to medium-high heat. In a medium bowl, combine ground chuck, curry powder, cumin, sugar, cilantro, chopped onion, chile, salt and black pepper, mixing lightly with hands until well blended. Form beef mixture into four patties and place patties on the grate. Cover grill and cook for 3 to 4 minutes undisturbed. Flip patties once, cover grill and continue to cook 3 to 4 additional minutes or until juices run clear and the internal temperature reaches 160°. Meanwhile, cut green onions or scallions into pieces, 3" long. Spray a 10" piece of aluminum foil with nonstick cooking spray and place on grate. Set onions and mushrooms on foil, brush with teriyaki sauce and grill until browned and softened. Place one beef patty inside each bun and top with grilled onions and mushrooms. Serve with additional teriyaki sauce, if desired.

CHEESE-STUFFED MEATBALL KEBABS

Makes 4 to 6 servings

1 egg, lightly beaten
⅓ C. grated Parmesan cheese
2 cloves garlic, minced
½ tsp. salt
⅛ tsp. black pepper
1 tsp. dried Italian seasoning
1½ lbs. lean ground beef
2 oz. fontina or mozzarella cheese, cubed
8 canned artichoke hearts, drained
1 (6 to 8 oz.) pkg. fresh cremini mushrooms
1 pt. grape tomatoes
Warm Balsamic Glaze*
Hot cooked rice

In a large bowl, combine egg, Parmesan cheese, garlic, salt, black pepper and Italian seasoning. Add ground beef and mix well, using hands as needed. Divide meatball mixture into approximately 16 portions. Shape each portion around one cheese cube to make meatballs. Thread meatballs, artichokes, mushrooms and tomatoes alternately on 16 (10") metal or soaked wooden skewers, leaving a small space between items.

To cook, lightly oil the grate and preheat grill to medium heat. Place kebabs on the grate and grill for 5 to 6 minutes or until meat is partially cooked. Transfer half of the Warm Balsamic Glaze into a small bowl for brushing. Turn kebabs and brush them with half of the glaze, continuing to grill for an additional 5 to 6 minutes or until meat is cooked through and internal temperature reaches 160°. Serve kebabs over rice and drizzle with remaining warmed glaze.

*Warm Balsamic Glaze: In a small saucepan over medium heat, combine ⅓ cup balsamic vinegar, 2 teaspoons olive oil, ½ teaspoon minced garlic, ¼ teaspoon salt, ⅛ teaspoon black pepper and ¼ teaspoon Italian seasoning. Bring mixture to a boil while stirring; reduce heat and simmer uncovered for 4 minutes or until reduced to about ¼ cup.

BEEF

Ground Beef

BASIC COOKING TIPS

Fully cooked cuts of pork should reach an internal temperature of 145° before eating to ensure safety. Let the meat stand for 3 minutes before carving/serving. When cooked correctly, the meat should be juicy and tender. Color is not an indication of doneness so the meat may retain a slightly pink color in the center. To shred pork roasts, it is often desirable to cook the meat until it reaches a higher internal temperature for added tenderness. Ground pork should be cooked to 160°.

	Cook to *this internal temperature*
Pork chops (½" to 1½" thick)	**145°**
Tenderloins	**145°**
Pork roast	**145° to 190°**
Ground pork	**160°**
Ham	**145°**
Reheating fully-cooked ham	**145°**
Fully cooked smoked pork chops	**145°**

PORK CHOPS

Pork chops are available with the bone in or boneless, and they may be purchased in different thicknesses, which affects cooking time. Generally, thin chops are less than ¾" thick and require a short grilling time over high heat. Chops thicker than ¾" should be cooked more slowly with lower heat so they can cook though without becoming dry inside. Smoked pork chops are fully cooked and have a flavor similar to ham so grilling time is shorter than regular pork chops.

PORK

Pork Chops

GRILLED PORK CHOPS

Makes 4 servings
- 1 tsp. ground cumin
- 1 tsp. mild chili powder
- Salt and black pepper to taste
- 1 T. olive oil
- 4 pork loin or rib chops, ¾" to 1" thick

Lightly oil the grate and preheat grill to medium heat*. In a small bowl, combine cumin, chili powder, salt and black pepper; mix well. Brush both sides of each pork chop with oil. Sprinkle with cumin mixture.

To cook, place chops on the grate and grill for 8 to 14 minutes, turning once. Adjust cooking time for thickness of meat; chops are done when browned on both sides and internal temperature reaches 160°.

* If grilling thinner pork chops, use medium-high heat and shorten grilling time to approximately 4 minutes per side.

Boneless pork chops may also be used. If you purchase thick boneless chops (1½"), try wrapping two strips of bacon around the outside edge of each chop and securing with toothpicks before marinating or grilling.

CUBAN RUB

Makes about ⅓ cup
- 2 T. grated lime peel
- 1 T. cumin seed
- 1 T. black pepper
- ½ tsp. salt
- 1 clove garlic, minced
- 2 T. olive oil

In a small bowl, combine lime peel, cumin, black pepper, salt, garlic and oil; mix well. Rub mixture evenly on both sides of pork chops. Grill as directed above.

Add flavor to any pork chop by using one of these rubs before grilling.

FAR EASTERN RUB

Makes about 3 tablespoons

1 T. dry mustard
1½ tsp. ground cumin
1½ tsp. curry powder
1½ tsp. Hungarian paprika
¾ tsp. salt
¼ tsp. cayenne pepper
1 tsp. black pepper
⅛ tsp. ground allspice
⅛ tsp. ground cloves

In a small bowl, combine dry mustard, cumin, curry powder, paprika, salt, cayenne pepper, black pepper, allspice and cloves; mix well. Rub or pat mixture over both sides of pork chops. Cover and refrigerate for 30 minutes or up to 2 hours. Grill chops as directed on page 64.

SPICY SOY SAUCE MARINADE

Marinates 4 pork chops

½ C. soy sauce
½ C. lime juice
1½ tsp. cayenne pepper
3 cloves garlic, minced

In a small bowl, mix soy sauce, lime juice, cayenne pepper and garlic. Reserve ¼ cup of the mixture for basting. Place pork chops in remaining marinade and refrigerate for 1 hour.

To cook, remove chops and discard marinade. Grill meat over medium heat for 2 minutes. Turn and baste with reserved marinade. Grill 10 to 14 minutes longer or until internal temperature reaches 160°, turning and basting again during cooking. (Shorten the time for thin chops.)

Use marinades with any pork chops. Brines are best for thick chops.

APPLE CIDER BRINE

Brines 4 thick pork chops

½ C. coarse salt (kosher or sea salt)
½ C. brown sugar
1 tsp. dried thyme
½ tsp. whole black peppercorns
½ tsp. whole cloves
2 C. unfiltered apple cider
1 C. ice cubes
Olive oil

In a large saucepan over medium heat, mix 1 cup water, salt, brown sugar, thyme, peppercorns and cloves; boil for 2 to 3 minutes until sugar and salt dissolve. Remove from heat; stir in cider and ice. Place pork chops in an extra-large resealable plastic bag. Pour brine over chops, seal bag and refrigerate for 6 to 12 hours.

To cook, lightly oil the grate and preheat grill to medium heat. Drain chops, rinse and pat dry; discard brine. Brush with oil and place over direct heat. Cover grill and cook for 12 to 16 minutes, turning once, or until internal temperature reaches 160°.

NECTARINE SALSA

Garnishes 4 pork chops

2 nectarines, pitted, peeled and diced
1 ripe tomato, seeded and diced
¼ C. diced onion
2 T. chopped fresh cilantro
2 T. lime juice
¼ tsp. crushed red pepper flakes, or to taste
Salt to taste

In a large bowl, combine nectarines, tomato, onion, cilantro, lime juice and red pepper flakes. Toss to blend and season with salt. Cover and refrigerate for 30 minutes to blend flavors. Serve with grilled pork chops.

AUTUMN PEAR RELISH

Garnishes 6 pork chops

1 grapefruit, peeled and segmented
2 pears, peeled, cored and diced
½ C. chopped cherries
2 T. chopped red onion
½ tsp. minced garlic
1 jalapeño pepper, seeded and chopped
½ tsp. finely grated lime peel
2 T. lime juice

Cut grapefruit segments into thirds and place pieces in a medium bowl. Add pears, cherries, onion, garlic, jalapeño pepper, lime peel and lime juice; toss well to blend. Serve with grilled pork chops.

PORK CHOP WITH PECAN STUFFING

Makes 6 servings

3 T. butter
½ C. coarsely chopped pecans
¼ C. sliced green onions
¼ C. chopped green bell pepper
¼ tsp. dried rosemary
⅛ tsp. white pepper
2 C. cubed stale bread
⅓ to ½ C. chicken broth
6 (1½" thick) pork loin chops, cut horizontally to create pockets

In a small skillet over medium heat, melt butter. Add pecans, onions and bell pepper; sauté until onions are tender. Stir in rosemary and white pepper; cook for 1 minute more. In a medium bowl, combine pecan mixture and bread cubes; toss with enough chicken broth to moisten. Spoon some stuffing into the pocket of each pork chop and secure edges with toothpicks.

To cook, lightly oil the grate and preheat grill for medium indirect heat. Place stuffed chops on the grate over indirect heat and grill for 50 to 60 minutes or until internal temperature reaches 160°, turning chops partway through cooking time. Remove toothpicks before serving.

Cut thick pork chops horizontally, from fatty edge toward bone, to create a pocket that will hold this delicious stuffing.

AUTUMN PORK CHOP STACKS

Makes 4 servings

4 (¾" to 1" thick) pork chops*
4 thick apple slices, unpeeled
4 thick sweet potato slices, peeled
4 thick red onion slices
½ tsp. dried savory
⅛ tsp. ground nutmeg
Salt and black pepper to taste
4 tsp. butter

In a nonstick skillet over medium-hot heat, lightly brown pork chops on both sides. Cut four (12") pieces of heavy-duty aluminum foil and spray the dull side of each piece with nonstick cooking spray. Place a pork chop in the center of each piece. Top each chop with one apple slice, one sweet potato slice and one red onion slice. Sprinkle some savory, nutmeg, salt and black pepper on each stack. Top each with a teaspoon of butter. Wrap the foil around the stacked foods, sealing edges well and allowing extra room for air to circulate.

To cook, preheat grill to medium heat. Place foil packs over coals and cook for 40 to 50 minutes or until meat is cooked through and vegetables are tender. Turn packs several times while grilling. Remove from grill and let packs rest for 5 minutes before carefully cutting open to eat.

BBQ Pork Foil Packs. *Make BBQ Pork Foil Packs with thin pork chops, 2" pieces of sweet corn on the ear, wedges of new potatoes and baby carrots sliced lengthwise. Omit the seasonings listed above, but mix together ½ cup bottled barbeque sauce, ¼ cup honey and 2 teaspoons ground cumin. Season with salt and pepper. Spoon 3 tablespoons of sauce over each serving, wrap in foil and grill packs over medium heat for 20 minutes, or until pork is almost cooked through, turning once. Remove from grill and let packs rest 5 minutes before cutting open to eat.*

* Shorten cooking time if using thin pork chops (½" to ¾" thick).

PORK TENDERLOIN

Pork tenderloin is very lean and mild-flavored so it benefits from the use of marinades and seasonings. Use a sharp knife to trim off silver skin from the tenderloin before grilling. Don't overcook tenderloins; remove meat from the grate early and allow some standing time for juices to redistribute.

PORK

Pork Tenderloin

PERFECT GRILLED PORK TENDERLOIN

Makes 6 to 8 servings

1 tsp. garlic powder
1 tsp. salt
¾ to 1 tsp. black pepper
2 (1 lb.) pork tenderloins
1 T. olive oil
1 C. bottled barbeque sauce, optional

In a small bowl, combine garlic powder, salt and black pepper; mix well. Sprinkle over all sides of pork and pat gently into meat. Brush meat lightly with oil and let stand while heating the grill.

To cook, lightly oil the grate and preheat grill to medium-high heat. Place tenderloins on the grate over heat and sear for 1 to 2 minutes on each side until browned. Reduce temperature and arrange to continue grilling with indirect heat. Move pork to cooler side of grill, close lid and cook for 25 to 30 minutes. Turn meat over, brush with barbeque sauce, if desired, and cook for 8 to 10 minutes longer, or until internal temperature nearly reaches 160°. Remove from grill and let stand under a foil tent for 5 minutes before slicing.

To prevent the narrow tenderloin ends from drying out on the grill, trim off the ends before grilling and slice them into smaller chunks. Grill the large pieces of tenderloin as directed above, but thread the chunks onto double skewers and grill them separately for a shorter period of time. If desired, slice thinly for use in fajitas.

Apple wood chips add a great smoked flavor to grilled pork tenderloin.

TANGY BBQ RUB

Makes about ½ cup

½ C. instant orange drink mix powder
1 tsp. cayenne pepper
½ tsp. paprika
1 tsp. garlic powder
½ tsp. ground allspice
½ tsp. onion salt

In a small bowl, combine orange drink powder, cayenne pepper, paprika, garlic powder, allspice and onion salt; mix well. Lightly rub mixture on pork tenderloin before grilling as directed on page 68. Sprinkle more of the mixture on meat after grilling, if desired. Store mixture in an airtight container.

This rub also works well on chicken.

CARIBBEAN SPICE RUB

Makes about ⅓ cup
4 tsp. ground nutmeg
4 tsp. ground cumin
4 tsp. garlic salt
1 T. ground cinnamon
¼ to ½ tsp. cayenne pepper

This spice rub tastes good with fruit salsas on the side.

In a small bowl, combine nutmeg, cumin, garlic salt, cinnamon and cayenne pepper; mix well. Sprinkle mixture over pork and pat into meat. Cover and refrigerate for 15 to 30 minutes before grilling as directed on page 68.

PINEAPPLE MARINADE

Marinates 2 lbs. pork tenderloin
⅓ C. pineapple juice
2 T. lime juice
2 cloves garlic, minced
2 tsp. cumin
⅓ C. vegetable oil
1 tsp. salt
¼ tsp. black pepper

In a large resealable plastic bag, combine pineapple juice, lime juice, garlic, cumin, oil, salt and pepper; mix well. Add tenderloin(s) to the bag, seal and turn to coat. Refrigerate to marinate pork for at least 1 hour or overnight. To cook, remove meat and discard marinade. Lightly oil the grate and preheat grill to medium heat. Place pork on the grate, cover grill and cook for 20 to 25 minutes, turning frequently, until internal temperature reaches 160°. Remove from heat and let stand 5 minutes under a foil tent before slicing.

FIRECRACKER MARINADE

Marinates 2 lbs. pork tenderloin
½ C. bottled barbeque sauce
2 T. brown sugar
2 T. olive oil
2 T. white wine vinegar
2 T. soy sauce
1 to 2 tsp. red pepper sauce
1 clove garlic, minced

In a large resealable plastic bag, combine barbeque sauce, brown sugar, oil, vinegar, soy sauce, red pepper sauce and garlic; mix well. Remove ¼ cup of marinade, cover and refrigerate for basting. Add pork to bag, seal, and turn to coat meat. Refrigerate to marinate meat for 2 to 12 hours, turning occasionally. To cook, remove meat and discard marinade. Grill tenderloin as directed for Pineapple Marinade above, using reserved Firecracker Marinade to brush meat several times during cooking. Discard any remaining marinade after grilling.

SWEET 'N' SASSY MARINADE

Marinates 2 lbs. pork tenderloin

⅓ C. honey
⅓ C. soy sauce
⅓ C. teriyaki sauce
3 T. brown sugar
1 T. minced gingerroot
3 cloves garlic, minced
1½ T. ketchup
½ tsp. onion powder
½ tsp. cinnamon
¼ tsp. cayenne pepper

In a medium bowl, combine honey, soy sauce, teriyaki sauce, brown sugar, gingerroot, garlic, ketchup, onion powder, cinnamon and cayenne pepper; mix well. Pour half of the marinade into a large resealable plastic bag. Add pork, seal, and turn to coat meat. Refrigerate to marinate pork for 4 to 8 hours, turning occasionally. Cover and refrigerate remaining half of marinade for basting. To cook, remove pork and discard marinade. Lightly oil the grate and preheat grill to medium-high heat, arranging for indirect cooking. Place pork on the grate over indirect heat for 20 to 25 minutes or until internal temperature reaches 160°. Baste meat frequently with reserved marinade and turn once. Remove from grill and let stand under a foil tent for 5 minutes before slicing.

MEDITERRANEAN MARINADE

Marinates 2 lbs. pork tenderloin

⅓ C. lemon juice
¼ C. olive oil
2 cloves garlic, minced
2 T. chopped fresh parsley
1 tsp. crumbled dried oregano
1 tsp. salt
¼ tsp. black pepper

In a large resealable plastic bag, combine lemon juice, oil, garlic, parsley, oregano, salt and black pepper; mix well. Add pork, seal and turn bag to coat meat. Refrigerate to marinate meat for at least 2 hours or overnight. To cook, remove meat and discard marinade. Grill tenderloin as directed above for Sweet 'n' Sassy Marinade.

FRUIT CRAZE SALSA

Garnishes 8 servings of pork tenderloin

2 C. diced assorted fresh fruit (cantaloupe, honeydew melon, grapes, papaya, mango)
1 T. chopped fresh cilantro
1 to 2 tsp. lime juice

In a small bowl, combine fruits, cilantro and lime juice; toss gently to blend. Cover and refrigerate for 30 minutes to blend flavors. Serve with grilled pork tenderloin or other pork dishes.

FRESH PINEAPPLE SALSA

Garnishes 8 servings of pork tenderloin

2 C. fresh pineapple, chopped
2 T. lime juice
½ C. chopped fresh cilantro
½ jalapeño pepper, seeded and chopped
½ tsp. crushed red pepper flakes
Salt to taste

In a blender or food processor container, combine pineapple, lime juice, cilantro, jalapeño pepper and red pepper flakes; pulse until ingredients are mixed well but still chunky. Transfer to a serving bowl and season with salt. Cover and refrigerate for 30 minutes to blend flavors.

This salsa also tastes good with grilled salmon.

PORK ROASTS

A pork shoulder roast or pork butt can be sliced or shredded for pork sandwiches. Making it tender requires long, slow cooking over indirect heat until it reaches a high internal temperature (180° to 190° if the meat will be pulled).

SMOKED PULLED PORK SANDWICHES

Makes 12 servings

1 (5 to 6 lb.) pork shoulder roast or pork butt
3 T. vegetable oil
2 T. salt
1 T. black pepper
2 T. paprika
1 tsp. cayenne pepper, optional
1 C. apple juice, optional
12 large sandwich buns or kaiser rolls, split
Sauce of choice

Trim excess fat, rinse meat and pat dry. Coat meat with oil. In a small bowl, combine salt, black pepper, paprika and optional cayenne pepper; mix well. Sprinkle pork with salt mixture and gently rub over meat. Cover meat in plastic wrap and refrigerate for 8 to 24 hours before grilling.

To cook, lightly oil the grate, preheat grill to medium-low heat (225° to 250°) and arrange for indirect cooking. Add a pouch of hickory chips to produce smoke. Place meat on the grate over cooler side of the grill and close lid. For the first 2 hours of grilling, check the heat every 30 minutes and add briquettes or adjust temperature to maintain heat and smoke. After 2 hours, transfer meat to a roasting rack inside a heavy-duty foil roasting pan and add 1 cup water (or apple juice). Cover pan tightly with foil. Increase grill temperature to 350° and cook for 2 to 3 hours or until internal temperature reaches 190°. Rotate pan occasionally. When a fork inserted into the meat turns easily, the meat is ready. Turn off heat and allow meat to rest for 20 to 30 minutes. Shred or slice the pork. Serve meat on buns with sauce or place shredded pork into the sauce and heat well before serving on buns.

EASY BBQ SAUCE

Makes about 3 cups

1 (18 oz.) bottled barbeque sauce
1 (8 oz.) can tomato sauce
¼ C. molasses
2 cloves garlic, minced

In a large saucepan, mix together barbeque sauce, tomato sauce, molasses and garlic. Reserve 1 cup of mixture for serving later. Add shredded pork to mixture in saucepan; cook on medium-low for 5 minutes or until heated through, stirring occasionally. Warm up the reserved sauce mixture and serve the shredded pork in buns with the sauce on the side.

CHUNKY BBQ SAUCE

Makes about 4½ cups
1 T. vegetable oil
1 Spanish onion, finely diced
1 jalapeño pepper, seeded and finely diced
2 fresh tomatoes, coarsely chopped
1 (14.2 oz.) can diced tomatoes
2 C. cider vinegar
¼ C. honey
½ C. brown sugar
1 T. Worcestershire sauce
Salt to taste

In a medium saucepan over medium-high heat, heat oil. Add onion and jalapeño pepper; sauté until soft. Add fresh and canned tomatoes with juices, vinegar, honey, brown sugar and Worcestershire sauce; cook until sugar dissolves and sauce is reduced and slightly thickened. Season with salt. Add sauce to shredded pork and mix well. Serve on buns.

GARLIC-SAGE RUB

Makes about ⅓ cup
8 cloves garlic, minced
3 T. chopped fresh sage
2 T. olive oil
½ tsp. salt
¼ tsp. black pepper

In a small bowl, combine garlic, sage, oil, salt and pepper; mix well. Rub garlic mixture over pork roast before grilling as directed on page 72.

This rub can also be used with grilled pork chops.

ALL-PURPOSE PORK RUB

Makes about ¼ cup
1 T. paprika
1½ tsp. salt
1½ tsp. sugar
1½ tsp. brown sugar
1½ tsp. ground cumin
1½ tsp. chili powder
1½ tsp. cayenne pepper
1½ tsp. black pepper

In a small bowl, combine paprika, salt, sugar, brown sugar, cumin, chili powder, cayenne pepper and black pepper. Sprinkle mixture over pork roast and rub in well before grilling as directed on page 72.

Use this rub with any cut of pork.

PORK RIBS

Traditional smoked ribs are grilled very slowly at a low temperature (225° to 240°) for optimal tenderness. When the meat flakes with a fork and is loose around the bones, the ribs are done. Although a barbeque smoker is the preferred method, a covered gas grill or charcoal grill with a drip pan can also be used. Pre-cooking ribs in water or apple juice tenderizes them and shortens grilling time. Simply simmer for about 1 hour, drain and let cool before marinating or rubbing. Then grill over medium heat for 20 to 30 minutes.

SUMMERTIME BARBEQUED RIBS

Makes 6 servings

¼ C. brown sugar
2 tsp. seasoned salt
2 tsp. chili powder
4 lbs. pork back ribs
¼ C. prepared yellow mustard
4 C. hickory or fruitwood chunks
¼ C. bottled barbeque sauce
Additional barbeque sauce

In a small bowl, combine brown sugar, seasoned salt and chili powder; set aside. Rinse ribs and remove membrane. If desired, cut ribs into serving pieces. Brush ribs with mustard and sprinkle with brown sugar mixture. Cover and refrigerate for 6 to 24 hours.

One hour before grilling, soak wood chunks in water. Remove the grate and lightly oil it. Preheat grill to medium heat. Place a drip pan holding 1" of water in the center and arrange hot coals around pan. Sprinkle damp wood over the coals before replacing grate. Place ribs, meaty side up, on the grate over the drip pan, but not over the coals. Cover the grill and cook ribs over indirect heat for 1¼ to 1½ hours or until tender. Add more coals and wood as needed. Brush ribs with ¼ cup barbeque sauce and grill for 5 minutes longer. Serve with additional barbeque sauce as desired. (If using very low heat on the charcoal grill, cook ribs for up to 3 hours.)

SWEET & SAVORY SAUCE

Makes about 1¾ cups

1 C. chili sauce
¾ C. grape jelly
1½ T. beef broth (or dry red wine)
1 tsp. Dijon mustard

In a small saucepan over medium heat, mix chili sauce, jelly, broth and Dijon mustard; heat and stir until jelly is melted. Remove half of sauce for basting; keep remaining sauce warm for serving. Baste ribs with sauce several times during the last part of cooking, turning occasionally. Serve reserved sauce with grilled ribs.

HONEY & ORANGE SAUCE

Makes about 5 cups

1 (29 oz.) can tomato sauce
⅔ C. honey
½ C. finely chopped onion
¼ C. soy sauce
¼ C. red wine vinegar
2 tsp. onion powder
2 tsp. finely shredded orange peel
1½ tsp. garlic powder
1½ tsp. ground ginger
1 tsp. barbeque seasoning

In a large saucepan over medium heat, combine tomato sauce, honey, onion, soy sauce, vinegar, onion powder, orange peel, garlic powder, ginger and barbeque seasoning. Simmer mixture for 10 minutes, stirring occasionally. Cool sauce. Pour 2¾ cups of sauce into a large resealable plastic bag. Add precooked ribs, seal and refrigerate for 4 to 24 hours. Reserve and refrigerate remaining sauce. To cook, remove ribs and discard marinade. Place ribs on the grate over direct medium heat and cook for 20 to 30 minutes, using ¼ cup of reserved sauce to baste ribs during grilling. Heat remaining sauce to serve alongside grilled ribs.

SLOW COOKER GRILLED RIBS

Makes about 6 servings

3½ lbs. pork back ribs
¼ C. brown sugar
1 tsp. salt
½ tsp. black pepper
3 T. liquid smoke
2 cloves garlic, minced
1 onion, sliced
½ C. carbonated cola beverage
1 C. bottled barbeque sauce

Spray the inside of a 4- to 5-quart slow cooker with nonstick cooking spray. Peel off the membrane from the underside of the ribs and rinse ribs. In a small bowl, combine brown sugar, salt, black pepper, liquid smoke and garlic; rub mixture into ribs. Cut ribs into 4" pieces. Layer the ribs and onion slices in slow cooker. Pour cola over the ribs, cover and cook on low heat setting for 8 to 9 hours or until tender.

To finish cooking on the grill, lightly oil the grate and preheat grill to medium heat. Place grate 4" to 6" above heat. Remove ribs from slow cooker; drain and discard liquid. Place ribs on the grate and brush with barbeque sauce. Cover the grill and cook for 15 minutes, turning once.

Ribs can also be precooked in a molasses sauce in a 6-quart Dutch oven. Combine 4 to 5 cups low-sodium beef broth with ½ cup molasses, ½ cup cider vinegar, 2 tablespoons prepared yellow mustard, 2 tablespoons Worcestershire sauce and ½ teaspoon hot sauce. Mix well and bring to a boil. Add 4 pounds of baby back ribs, cover, reduce heat and simmer for 20 minutes. To finish cooking on the grill, place ribs on the grate over low heat and cover with foil. Grill for about 2 hours, turning every 20 minutes. During the last 20 minutes of grilling, remove foil, then brush ribs with molasses sauce and turn twice. Discard remaining sauce.

HAM & SMOKED PORK CHOPS

Fully-cooked ham and smoked pork chops grill quickly since they just need to be heated through to 145°. If a label indicates the ham must be "cooked thoroughly", grill it to an internal temperature of 160°. Avoid over-cooking ham and smoked pork chops, which will dry out the meat.

PORK

Ham & Smoked Pork Chops

GRILLED HAM STEAK (OR SMOKED PORK CHOPS)

Makes 4 servings

1 (1 to 2 lb.) center-cut ham steak or 4 (1" thick) boneless smoked pork chops

Lightly oil the grate and preheat grill to medium heat. Place ham or smoked pork chops on the grate and cook for 6 to 10 minutes*, turning once halfway through grilling. If desired, brush with Orange-Apricot Glaze (recipe below) and continue to cook until heated through. To serve ham, place meat on a platter and garnish with a sauce over the top. Cut ham into individual servings.

* Bone-in, thick-cut ham steak and smoked pork chops generally require the full 10 minutes of grilling time. Thinner steaks will cook more quickly.

ORANGE-APRICOT GLAZE

Makes about ¾ cup

¼ C. apricot preserves
¼ C. orange juice
2 T. soy sauce
1 T. lime juice

In a small bowl, combine preserves, orange juice, soy sauce and lime juice; mix well. Grill each side of smoked pork chops or ham steak for several minutes. Brush with the glaze and cook on both sides until heated through.

MAPLE-MUSTARD GLAZE

Makes about ¼ cup

3 T. Dijon mustard
1 T. maple syrup

In a small bowl, whisk together Dijon mustard and syrup until blended. Grill each side of smoked pork chops or ham steak for several minutes. Brush with the glaze and continue to cook on both sides until golden brown. Drizzle remaining glaze over grilled meat before serving.

PEACH CHUTNEY

Garnishes 4 to 6 servings

1 (15 oz.) can sliced peaches, drained
¾ C. cider vinegar
½ C. brown sugar
½ C. minced onion
1 apple, peeled, cored and chopped
1 tsp. pickling spice
1 T. lemon juice

Coarsely chop peaches. In a large saucepan over medium-low heat, combine peaches, vinegar, brown sugar, onion, apple, pickling spice and lemon juice. Simmer for 20 minutes or until slightly thickened. Cool, cover and refrigerate. Serve cold or at room temperature over ham or smoked pork chops.

CRANBERRY CHUTNEY

Garnishes 4 to 6 servings

1 onion, chopped
1 T. vegetable oil
2 C. fresh cranberries, rinsed
¾ C. sugar
1½ T. dry mustard
⅛ tsp. ground cloves
⅛ tsp. ground cinnamon
⅛ tsp. ground mace

In a large skillet over medium heat, sauté onion in oil until tender. Stir in 1 cup water, cranberries and sugar; boil for 1 minute. Stir in dry mustard, cloves, cinnamon and mace. Reduce heat and keep warm until serving. Sauce may be made ahead and refrigerated to serve cold or at room temperature.

Jalapeño Cherry Sauce. Try a Jalapeño Cherry Sauce by boiling 1 (14 ounce) can sweet pitted cherries with 1 cup jalapeño jelly and ½ teaspoon ground coriander. Serve warm over ham.

CLASSIC CHERRY GLAZE

Makes about 2 cups

1 (12 oz.) jar cherry preserves
¼ C. honey
¼ C. red wine vinegar
¼ tsp. ground nutmeg
¼ tsp. ground cinnamon
¼ tsp. ground cloves
¼ tsp. salt

In a small saucepan over medium-low heat, combine preserves, honey, vinegar, nutmeg, cinnamon, cloves and salt; mix well. Bring mixture to a simmer and cook for 5 minutes, stirring often. Grill one side of ham steak or smoked pork chops for several minutes, then turn and brush with glaze. Grill for 3 minutes, turn again and brush with more cherry glaze. Cook for 1 to 2 minutes more or until ham is glazed and heated through. Serve with any remaining cherry glaze.

GROUND PORK

Ground pork, like ground beef, is easy to prepare and cook on the grill. The internal temperature should reach 160° before serving. To keep burgers flat during grilling, make a thumb indentation, ½" deep, in the center of each patty before placing on the grill.

SIMPLE PORK BURGERS

Makes 4 to 6 servings

1½ lbs. lean ground pork
¼ tsp. garlic powder
¼ tsp. onion powder
¼ C. minced red onion, optional
Barbeque sauce of choice
4 hamburger buns or soft onion rolls, split

Lightly oil the grate and preheat grill to medium-high heat. In a medium bowl, combine ground pork, garlic powder, onion powder and optional onion; mix well using hands as needed. Form meat mixture into four to six patties, ¾" to 1" thick. Make a thumb indentation in the center of each patty and place on the grate over direct heat. Cook for 12 to 16 minutes, turning once and brushing with barbeque sauce toward the end of grilling. Meat should be cooked through with an internal temperature of 160°. Brush additional barbeque sauce on both sides of cooked pork patties just before serving on buns or rolls.

HONEY OF A BARBEQUE SAUCE

Makes about 3 cups

2 C. white vinegar
¾ C. ketchup
1 C. Western salad dressing
¼ C. honey
¼ C. sugar
1½ tsp. lemon juice
1 tsp. cayenne pepper (or less to taste)
1½ tsp. black pepper
¼ tsp. salt

1½ tsp. liquid smoke, optional

In a large saucepan over low heat, combine vinegar, ketchup, dressing, honey, sugar, lemon juice, cayenne pepper, black pepper and salt. Simmer until sauce is thick and creamy, about 1 hour. If desired, add liquid smoke during the last 30 minutes of simmering. Serve with grilled pork burgers. Store leftover sauce in an airtight container in the refrigerator.

This sauce tastes good with other grilled pork or beef recipes.

BUTTERMILK BBQ SAUCE

Makes about 1 cup

1 C. apple cider
1 T. brown sugar
½ C. bottled barbeque sauce
1 T. buttermilk

In a medium saucepan over medium-low heat, combine cider and brown sugar; mix well. Bring mixture to a simmer and cook for 25 minutes. Reduce heat to low and add barbeque sauce, stirring well. When heated through, remove from heat and add buttermilk, stirring well to incorporate. Serve with grilled pork burgers.

Try this sauce over grilled pork chops, too.

GRILLED PINEAPPLE RELISH

Tops 4 to 6 burgers

4 to 5 pineapple rings
4 green onions
Olive oil
½ jalapeño pepper, seeded and diced
1 T. lime juice
2 tsp. honey
1 T. chopped fresh cilantro

Lightly oil the grate and preheat grill to medium heat. Place pineapple rings on the grate and cook for 6 to 8 minutes, turning once, until heated through. Brush onions with oil and grill over medium heat for 4 minutes, turning once, until browned on both sides. Cut grilled pineapple into chunks and slice the grilled onions. Combine pineapple and onion in a bowl with jalapeño pepper, lime juice, honey and cilantro. Stir to blend and allow relish to rest for 30 minutes to blend flavors. Spoon some relish on top of grilled pork patties on buns.

APPLE COLESLAW

Tops 4 to 6 burgers

1 Granny Smith apple, cored and finely diced
2 C. shredded cabbage
¼ C. shredded carrot
2 T. chopped green bell pepper
1½ tsp. cider vinegar
½ tsp. salt
½ tsp. black pepper

In a medium bowl, combine apple, cabbage, carrot and bell pepper; mix well. Add vinegar, salt and black pepper, stirring for 1 minute or until blended. Cover bowl and refrigerate for at least 2 hours. Top grilled pork patties with Apple Coleslaw before serving, or serve it on the side.

GRILLED PEANUTTY-PORK BURGERS

Makes 4 servings

½ C. finely chopped onion
¼ C. finely chopped dry roasted peanuts
1 T. snipped fresh cilantro
1 T. grated fresh gingerroot
4 cloves garlic, minced, divided
¼ tsp. crushed red pepper flakes
1 tsp. salt
1 lb. lean ground pork
1 T. sesame oil
⅓ C. bottled chili sauce or Asian sweet
   chili sauce
1 T. creamy peanut butter
4 French rolls or hamburger buns, split
1 C. shredded bok choy
Additional chopped peanuts

Lightly oil the grate and preheat grill to medium heat. In a medium bowl, combine onion, ¼ cup peanuts, cilantro, gingerroot, 3 cloves garlic, red pepper flakes and salt. Add ground pork and mix well, using hands as needed. Shape mixture into four ½" thick patties. Brush patties with oil; cover and set aside. Place patties directly over heat and cook for 5 to 7 minutes. (If using a gas grill, cover grill during cooking.) Flip patties once and continue to cook for 5 to 6 minutes more or until meat is done and internal temperature reaches 160°.

Meanwhile, in a small bowl, whisk together chili sauce, peanut butter and remaining 1 clove minced garlic; set aside. Before serving, toast rolls on grill. Place a portion of the bok choy on the bottom of each roll and top with a grilled patty, some sauce mixture, additional chopped peanuts and bun top.

HOT DOGS & BRATS

Bratwurst can be purchased fully-cooked or raw and the label should tell you what type it is. Fully-cooked brats can be placed directly on a grill until heated through, but fresh raw bratwurst needs to be fully cooked on the inside without becoming burned on the outside. To accomplish this easily, simmer raw brats in a liquid such as water, cider or beer before browning them on the grill. This method can also be done with hot dogs.

GRILLED HOT DOGS

Makes 8 servings

  1 (8 ct.) pkg. hot dogs
  8 hot dog buns, split
  Condiments: ketchup, mustard, pickle relish, chopped onions

Lightly oil the grate and preheat grill to medium heat. Arrange hot dogs on the grate and grill them for 5 to 7 minutes, turning often, or until heated through and brown grill marks show. Place hot dogs in buns and dress them with condiments as desired.

To get crisp, well-blistered hot dogs that are fully heated inside, place them in a large saucepan and barely cover with water. Bring to a boil, cover the pan and remove it from the heat; let hot dogs stand in hot water for 5 minutes. With tongs, transfer the dogs to the grate and finish cooking on the grill for 3 to 5 minutes, turning several times, until browned.

BRATS & KRAUT

Makes 6 servings

  6 raw bratwurst
  1 onion, sliced
  1 (14.4 oz.) can shredded sauerkraut, drained
  1½ C. apple cider
  6 hoagie rolls or large hot dog buns, split
  Condiments: yellow or spicy brown mustard, ketchup, pickle relish, caraway seeds

Preheat the grill to medium heat. Place bratwurst in a single layer in a heavy-duty foil pan. If desired, arrange onion and sauerkraut over bratwurst*. Pour apple cider into pan and set pan on grate directly over the heat. Cover grill and cook for 20 to 25 minutes or until brats are cooked through without splitting the skins. Use tongs to transfer bratwurst to the grate; finish cooking directly over heat for 3 to 5 minutes, turning several times, or until brown grill marks show. Warm the rolls or buns on the grill. To serve, place a grilled bratwurst in each bun and top with sauerkraut mixture. Add condiments as desired and sprinkle with a few caraway seeds.

* To omit the sauerkraut and onion, simply simmer bratwurst in the apple cider for 15 minutes before transferring brats to the grate to brown and finish cooking.

To cook fresh bratwurst directly on the grill, use medium indirect heat and place brats on the grate over a drip pan. (Hickory chips may be added.) Cover the grill to slow-cook the brats for 30 to 40 minutes or until golden brown and cooked through. Move brats over direct heat near the end of cooking, turning several times, to get darker grill marks.

TOPPERS FOR HOT DOGS AND BRATS

PORK

Hot Dogs & Brats

Cobb Dog

Arrange chopped cobb or iceberg lettuce, fresh tomato chunks and crumbled bacon bits over grilled hot dogs or brats and drizzle with blue cheese dressing.

Southwestern Sizzle

While hot dogs or brats are cooking, grill several poblano chiles until skin is charred. Place into a bowl and cover to steam. Peel off skin and chop up chiles. Top grilled hot dogs or brats with chopped chiles and Monterey Jack cheese.

California Dream

Spread buns with a little mayonnaise, add grilled hot dogs or brats, and top with ripe avocado slices and fresh tomato chunks.

Royal Reuben

Spread buns with Russian salad dressing. Add grilled hot dogs or brats and top with thin slices of Swiss cheese and warm sauerkraut.

Tasty Texan

Add slices of longhorn Cheddar cheese and chopped onions on top of grilled hot dogs or brats with a drizzle of barbeque sauce.

Jamaican Jazz

Sauté thinly sliced onions in olive oil until tender. Dress the grilled hot dogs or brats with diced fresh mango, diced habanero chile pepper, sautéed onions and a sprinkling of jerk seasoning.

Viva la Paris

Top grilled hot dogs or brats with warm Brie cheese and sliced fresh pears.

Try any of these toppings to make hot dogs and brats interesting!

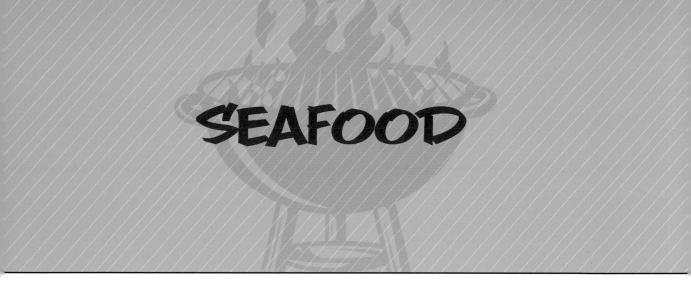

SEAFOOD

BASIC COOKING TIPS

Some fish are fragile and don't cook well on a grill; avoid very thin, flat fish, such as sole or flounder. Cooking time for seafood will depend upon the thickness of each piece, but like other foods, seafood continues to cook after being removed from the heat. To avoid overcooking, take fish off the grate when the center begins to turn opaque and the thickest part starts to flake when pressed with a fork. Brush both the seafood and grate lightly with canola oil to prevent sticking. A seafood basket makes grilling any type of seafood easy. Leaving the skin on fresh fish will help it stay together during grilling; remove it just before serving, if desired. Whereas tongs work well for turning beef or pork, spatulas work better for most seafood. Fish steaks are crosswise cuts, about 1" thick, through the fish's backbone. Fillets come from the sides of the fish and generally have the skin and bones removed. Fillets can be purchased as an entire half of the fish or cut into single serving pieces.

	Cook to *this internal temperature*
Most Fish	**145°**

SALMON

Salmon is a moderately firm fish with a mild to moderate flavor that cooks well on a grill. Fresh salmon steaks are especially tasty.

GRILLED SALMON

Makes 4 servings

   2 tsp. finely grated lemon peel
   1 tsp. ground cumin
   ½ tsp. salt
   ¼ tsp. black pepper
   4 (4 to 6 oz.) salmon filets (¾" to 1" thick)
   Lemon slices, optional

Lightly oil the grate and preheat grill to medium heat. In a small bowl, combine lemon peel, cumin, salt and black pepper; mix well. Sprinkle mixture over salmon. Lightly spray both sides of salmon fillets with nonstick cooking spray.

   To cook, arrange salmon fillets on the grate directly over the heat. Cover the grill and cook for 8 to 12 minutes, turning once halfway through grilling. Salmon is done when it is tender and flakes easily with a fork. Garnish with lemon slices, if desired.

SALMON SEASONING RUB

Makes about ¼ cup

   2 T. olive oil
   1 T. mild chili powder
   1 T. lime juice
   ¼ tsp. coarse salt
   ⅛ tsp. black pepper

In a small bowl, combine oil, chili powder, lime juice, salt and black pepper; mix well. Rub the spice mixture generously over each salmon fillet. Grill salmon as directed.

SWEET & SPICY RUB

Makes about ¼ cup

   2 T. brown sugar
   1 T. chili powder
   1 tsp. ground cumin
   ½ tsp. cayenne pepper, optional
   Pinch of salt and black pepper
   Olive oil

In a small bowl, combine brown sugar, chili powder, cumin, cayenne pepper, salt and black pepper; mix well. Rub each salmon fillet with olive oil and sprinkle spice mixture evenly over each piece, pressing lightly into salmon. Grill salmon as directed.

TOMATO-PARSLEY BASTING SAUCE

Bastes 4 salmon fillets

½ C. sun-dried tomato dressing
¼ C. chopped fresh parsley
¼ C. chopped sun-dried tomatoes

In a small bowl, combine dressing, parsley and tomatoes; mix well. Grill salmon for 6 minutes as directed on page 84; then turn and brush with dressing mixture. Grill for 5 to 8 minutes longer or until fish flakes easily with a fork.

LEMON-DILL MARINADE

Marinates 4 salmon fillets

⅓ C. olive oil
¼ C. lemon juice
2 T. chopped fresh dillweed
1 tsp. grated lemon peel
¼ tsp. salt
¼ tsp. black pepper

In a small bowl, whisk together oil, lemon juice, dillweed, lemon peel, salt and black pepper. Reserve 3 tablespoons; cover and refrigerate for basting later. Pour remaining marinade into a shallow baking dish and add salmon. Use tongs to turn fillets until well-coated. Cover dish and refrigerate to marinate salmon for up to 30 minutes. To cook, remove salmon and discard marinade. Grill salmon as directed on page 84, using reserved marinade to baste fish several times during grilling.

STRAWBERRY-AVOCADO SALSA

Garnishes 6 to 8 servings

½ C. pineapple chunks
1 T. pineapple juice
½ avocado, pitted, peeled and diced
2 C. strawberries, sliced
½ to 1 jalapeño pepper, seeded and
 finely chopped
1½ tsp. balsamic vinegar
¼ tsp. onion salt

In a medium bowl, combine pineapple chunks and juice, avocado, strawberries, jalapeño pepper, vinegar and onion salt; toss gently. Let mixture stand for 5 to 10 minutes to blend flavors. Serve over grilled salmon or other fish.

This salsa also tastes good over grilled chicken.

CANTALOUPE SALSA

Garnishes 4 to 6 servings

¼ large cantaloupe, peeled and cut into ½" cubes
2 T. fresh minced parsley
¼ C. fresh minced cilantro
¼ C. minced red onion
1½ tsp. lemon juice
1 tsp. olive oil
2 T. nonfat plain Greek yogurt

In a medium mixing bowl, combine cantaloupe, parsley, cilantro and onion. Toss with lemon juice, oil and yogurt. Chill for at least 2 hours before serving alongside grilled salmon or other fish.

Try this salsa with other grilled seafood or chicken.

CEDAR PLANKED SALMON

Makes 6 servings

3 (12") untreated cedar planks
⅓ C. vegetable oil
1 tsp. sesame oil
1½ T. rice vinegar
⅓ C. soy sauce
¼ C. chopped green onions
1 T. grated fresh gingerroot
1 tsp. minced garlic
2 (2 lb.) salmon fillets, skin removed (about 1" thick)

Soak cedar planks in warm water for 4 to 24 hours. In a shallow glass baking dish, combine vegetable oil, sesame oil, vinegar, soy sauce, onions, gingerroot and garlic; mix well. Place salmon in the marinade and turn to coat well. Cover and refrigerate to marinate for 15 to 60 minutes.

To cook, lightly oil the grate and preheat grill to medium heat. Place wet planks on the grate; boards are heated and ready for cooking when they start to smoke and make a crackling sound. Lightly brush the planks with oil using a paper towel and tongs. Place salmon fillets on the planks and discard marinade. Cover grill and cook for about 20 minutes or until fish flakes easily with a fork.

You may reuse planks if they are not too charred; just wash with warm water and let air dry.

HALIBUT & OTHER FISH

Use these recipes to grill halibut or other types of fish firm enough to cook on the grill, such as red snapper, haddock and orange roughy. These sauces and glazes add the finishing touch to all kinds of grilled fish.

GRILLED HALIBUT

Makes 4 servings
- 1¼ lbs. fresh or frozen halibut steaks or other fish (1" thick)
- 1 tsp. olive oil
- 3 cloves garlic, minced
- ¼ tsp. salt
- ¼ tsp. black pepper
- Cherry or yellow pear-shaped tomato halves, optional
- Fresh chives, optional

Thaw fish if frozen. Rinse fish and pat dry with paper towels. Cut into four serving-size pieces if necessary. In a small bowl, combine oil, garlic, salt and black pepper; mix well. Spread mixture evenly over fish, rubbing it in with fingers.

To cook, lightly oil the grate and preheat grill to medium heat. Place fish on the grate and grill, uncovered, for 8 to 12 minutes or until fish flakes easily with a fork, turning once during cooking. Garnish with tomato halves and chives, if desired.

MUSTARD LEMON BUTTER GLAZE

Makes about ⅓ cup
- 2 T. butter
- 2 T. lemon juice
- 1 T. Dijon mustard
- ½ tsp. dried, crushed basil (or 2 tsp. snipped fresh basil)

In a small saucepan over low heat, combine butter, lemon juice, Dijon mustard and basil; heat and stir until melted and well combined. Brush both sides of fish with butter mixture and grill as directed.

LEMON MAYONNAISE

Makes about ⅔ cup
- ½ C. mayonnaise
- ¼ C. light sour cream
- 2 T. snipped fresh flat-leaf parsley
- 2 tsp. finely grated lemon peel
- 2 tsp. lemon juice
- ¼ tsp. black pepper

In a small bowl, combine mayonnaise, sour cream, parsley, lemon peel, lemon juice and black pepper; mix well. Cover and chill for 30 minutes before serving with grilled fish.

PECAN BUTTER

Makes about ¾ cup

½ C. butter
½ C. finely chopped pecans

In a small saucepan over medium-high heat, melt butter. Stir in pecans and cook until toasted and butter becomes dark brown, without burning. Serve on grilled fish or other seafood.

DILLED CUCUMBER BUTTER

Makes about ¾ cup

½ C. butter
½ C. peeled, seeded and chopped cucumber
1 tsp. dried chives
½ tsp. dried dillweed
Salt to taste
Lemon juice to taste

In a small saucepan over medium-high heat, melt butter. Stir in cucumber, chives and dillweed; cook until heated through, 3 to 5 minutes. Season with salt and lemon juice. Serve on grilled seafood.

CURRY BUTTER

Makes about ½ cup

½ C. butter
2 T. finely chopped onion
1 tsp. snipped fresh dillweed
1 to 1½ tsp. curry powder
Dash garlic powder

In a small saucepan over medium-high heat, melt butter. Stir in onion, dillweed, curry powder and garlic powder. Cook for 5 minutes. Serve on grilled fish or shrimp.

Flavored butters can be used with any type of fish or seafood. Make them ahead of time and store in the refrigerator for up to 2 weeks.

HALIBUT & APPLE KEBABS

Makes 4 servings

1½ lbs. halibut (or cod or red snapper)
1 red onion
1 yellow or red apple, cored
1 sweet red or green bell pepper, cored
   and seeded
½ C. unsweetened apple juice
2 T. lime juice
2 T. olive oil
2 T. finely diced onion
½ tsp. dried thyme
1 tsp. salt
¼ tsp. black pepper

Rinse halibut and pat dry. Cut the fish, red onion, apple and bell pepper into 1" pieces; set aside. In a small bowl, combine apple juice, lime juice, oil, diced onion, thyme, salt and black pepper; mix well. Divide the marinade mixture between two large resealable plastic bags. Add halibut pieces to one bag; seal and turn to coat fish. Add onion, apple and bell pepper to the second bag; seal and turn to coat pieces. Refrigerate bags to marinate fish and apple mixture for 4 to 6 hours, turning occasionally.

To cook, lightly oil the grate and preheat grill to medium heat. Remove fish and discard marinade. Remove fruit and vegetables and reserve that marinade for basting. On eight metal or soaked wooden skewers, alternately thread pieces of fish, onion, apple and bell pepper as desired. Place skewers on the grate over direct heat. Cook uncovered for 6 to 10 minutes, turning once, until fish flakes easily with a fork and fruit and vegetables are tender. Baste frequently during grilling with reserved marinade.

The apple juice mixture may also be used to marinate whole halibut steaks or pieces before grilling.

TUNA

Fresh tuna is very lean so avoid overcooking or it will dry out. It can be grilled until fully cooked or just seared on both sides over high heat for a short time, leaving it very rare inside. Grilled tuna should be served immediately after removing from the grill.

GRILLED TUNA STEAKS

Makes 4 servings

4 (6 oz.) fresh tuna steaks (¾" to 1" thick)
3 T. olive oil
½ C. hickory or mesquite wood chips, soaked, optional
Salt and black pepper to taste
Garlic powder to taste, optional
Juice of 1 lime

Place tuna steaks in a large resealable plastic bag and add oil; seal bag and turn gently to coat fish. Refrigerate to marinate tuna for 1 hour.

To cook, lightly oil the grate and preheat grill to medium heat. If using charcoal, scatter wet wood chips on hot coals around outside edges. Remove tuna from the bag and season with salt, black pepper and optional garlic powder. Place fish on the grate, cover grill and cook for 6 to 10 minutes, turning once halfway through grilling. Drizzle with lime juice just before serving.

To make Blackened Grilled Tuna Steaks: Stir together 1 tablespoon dry mustard, 2 tablespoons dried cilantro, 1 tablespoon chili powder, 1 teaspoon black pepper and 1 teaspoon black mustard seeds. Coat fish with oil and sprinkle seasoning mixture over steaks; wrap and refrigerate for 2 to 3 hours. Grill for 8 minutes over hot coals, turning once halfway through cooking.

LIME & SOY SAUCE

Garnishes 4 tuna or halibut steaks

¼ C. olive oil
2 T. lime juice
1 tsp. soy sauce
1 T. white wine vinegar or rice vinegar

In a small bowl, whisk together oil, lime juice, vinegar and soy sauce until blended. Spoon mixture over grilled tuna steaks before serving.

ROASTED PEPPER SAUCE

Garnishes 4 tuna or halibut steaks
2 roasted sweet red bell peppers*
2 T. lime juice
2 tsp. chopped fresh thyme or dillweed
¼ tsp. salt
⅛ tsp. black pepper
1 T. butter

In a blender container or food processor, combine roasted peppers, lime juice, thyme, salt, black pepper and 2 tablespoons water. Cover and blend until smooth. Pour mixture into a small saucepan and cook over low heat until hot; stir in butter until melted. Drizzle warm pepper sauce onto four serving plates and top with grilled tuna steaks.

* To roast, rinse whole peppers and place them on a lightly-oiled grate over medium heat. Grill for 5 to 7 minutes per side, until skins are blistered and browned. Transfer peppers from the grill to an airtight container to steam as they cool. When cool, peel off skins and remove seeds and stem; cut into pieces.

GRILLED TUNA SANDWICHES

Makes 4 servings
2 T. soy sauce
1 T. sesame oil
1 T. orange juice
½ tsp. ground ginger
3 T. mayonnaise
4 (4 oz.) fresh tuna steaks (about ½" thick)
4 hamburger buns or kaiser rolls, split
Lettuce leaves
1 large tomato, sliced
Cucumber slices

In an 8" square baking dish, blend together soy sauce, oil, orange juice and ginger; remove 1 tablespoon of the mixture and stir it into the mayonnaise in a small bowl; cover and refrigerate for later use. Add tuna to remaining mixture in dish and turn to coat fish. Cover and refrigerate to marinate tuna at least 15 minutes or up to 2 hours.

To cook, lightly coat the grate with oil and preheat grill to medium heat. Remove tuna from dish and discard marinade. Place tuna on the grate over heat and grill for about 10 minutes or until fish flakes easily with a fork, turning once. To serve, spread reserved flavored mayonnaise on the cut sides of each bun; add lettuce, grilled tuna, tomato and cucumber to make sandwiches.

TROUT

Foil packs work well for fish that might fall apart if placed directly on the grate, such as trout, perch or tilapia. Spray the inside of the foil with nonstick cooking spray before arranging food.

Add 1 to 2 tablespoons of liquid before sealing to steam-cook the fish. White wine, lemon juice, broth and water are good choices. Fish foil packs do not need to be flipped during grilling.

FISH IN A FOIL PACK

Makes 4 servings

2 rainbow trout fillets or another tender fish*
   (about 1 lb.)
1 T. vegetable oil
Garlic salt to taste
Black pepper to taste
Paprika to taste
1 jalapeño pepper, seeded, sliced
1 lemon, sliced

* Try fillets of bass, flounder, perch or tilapia.

Preheat the grill to medium heat. Rinse fish and pat dry with paper towels. Rub fillets with oil and season with garlic salt, black pepper and paprika. Place each fillet on a 15" piece of sprayed aluminum foil. Top with jalapeño pepper slices and squeeze the juice from the ends of the lemon over the fish. Arrange lemon slices on top of fillets. Carefully fold all edges of foil to enclose fish and form a flat, airtight pack. Place foil packs on the grate over heat and cook for 15 to 20 minutes, without turning foil pack over, until fish flakes easily with a fork.

WITH OTHER INGREDIENTS

Add other ingredients to fish foil packs so each serving suits different tastes. Salmon may also be prepared this way.

Place one fish fillet on each piece of sprayed foil. Add 1 to 2 tablespoons of liquid and any of these ingredients before sealing the foil packs well. Leave some space for air to circulate when other foods are included.

Use 2 to 4 tablespoons (or equivalents) of any of these ingredients, alone or in desired combinations:

- diced carrots
- diced celery
- chopped or sliced yellow or green onions
- pineapple chunks
- diced green or red bell pepper
- sliced baby corn
- diced or sliced zucchini or butternut squash
- diced sweet potato
- fresh green beans, cut into 1" pieces

- orange or lemon slices
- grapefruit sections
- apple slices
- fresh or frozen drained spinach leaves
- grape tomatoes, halved
- sun-dried tomatoes
- shiitake mushrooms
- fresh asparagus

Seasonings and sauces to try:

- Seasonings such as dried oregano, dillweed, parsley, grated ginger, ground cinnamon or chopped fresh cilantro.

- Dressings such as prepared sun-dried tomato vinaigrette dressing, sesame-ginger, balsamic vinaigrette or Italian salad dressing.

- Condiments such as capers, black or green olives, honey, red pepper sauce, brown sugar or maple syrup, combinations of butter with olive oil, butter with lemon juice or white wine with cream.

SHRIMP

Grill raw shrimp for 2 to 4 minutes per side or until shrimp turn pink. To prevent the shrimp from falling through the grate or twisting on the skewers, try threading them on two parallel skewers before grilling. Marinating shrimp adds flavor and can prevent sticking to the grate.

GRILLED SHRIMP SKEWERS

Makes 4 servings

¼ C. balsamic vinaigrette dressing*, divided
1 lb. large raw shrimp, peeled, deveined
   and rinsed
1 red onion, cut into 1" pieces
1 lemon, cut into 8 wedges

Pour 2 tablespoons dressing into a large resealable plastic bag; add shrimp and toss until coated. Refrigerate to marinate shrimp for 10 minutes.

To cook, lightly oil the grate and preheat grill to medium-high heat. Remove shrimp and discard marinade. Thread shrimp and onion pieces alternately onto four (or eight) metal or soaked wooden skewers, placing a lemon wedge on each end. Pour remaining 2 tablespoons dressing into a small bowl and brush the dressing over the shrimp and onions. Place skewers on the grate and grill uncovered for 5 to 8 minutes or until shrimp turn pink, flipping occasionally. If desired, serve kebabs with sauces, relishes or salsas.

* In place of balsamic vinaigrette dressing, make your own shrimp marinade by combining ¼ cup olive oil with 1 teaspoon minced garlic. Then toss marinated shrimp in seasoned breadcrumbs until coated and grill until crumb coating browns and shrimp are cooked through.

ITALIAN SHRIMP MARINADE

Marinates 1½ lbs. shrimp

¼ C. olive oil
2 T. lemon juice
3 garlic cloves, minced
1 T. minced fresh rosemary
½ tsp. coarse salt
¼ tsp. black pepper

In a large resealable plastic bag, combine oil, lemon juice, garlic, rosemary, salt and black pepper; mix well. Add shrimp, seal bag and turn to coat. Refrigerate bag to marinate shrimp for 15 minutes. To cook, remove shrimp and discard marinade. Thread shrimp on skewers and cook as directed.

MANGO-GINGER MARINADE & SAUCE

Marinates 1 lb. shrimp
- ½ C. mango chutney
- 3 T. lime juice
- 1 tsp. grated fresh gingerroot
- ½ tsp. curry powder

In a large resealable plastic bag, combine chutney, lime juice, ginger and curry powder; mix well. Add shrimp, seal bag and turn to coat. Refrigerate bag to marinate shrimp for at least 15 minutes. To cook, remove shrimp and discard marinade. Thread shrimp on skewers and cook as directed on page 94.

Make another batch of this sauce to serve over shrimp placed in pita halves with torn lettuce and tomato chunks.

Try one of these marinades in place of the vinaigrette dressing before grilling the shrimp as directed on page 94.

SWEET & SOUR BBQ SAUCE

Makes about 3¼ cups
- 2 T. olive oil
- 2 T. minced garlic
- 1 C. honey
- ¼ C. soy sauce
- ½ C. balsamic vinegar
- 1 C. ketchup
- ¼ C. fresh brewed coffee
- ½ tsp. vanilla extract

In a medium saucepan over medium-low heat, place oil. Add garlic and cook until golden brown, stirring often. Wisk in honey, soy sauce, vinegar, ketchup and coffee. Simmer for 15 minutes. Stir in vanilla just before serving with grilled shrimp. If desired, reserve ¼ cup of mixture to baste shrimp during grilling.

MARMALADE DIPPING SAUCE

Makes about ½ cup
- ½ C. orange marmalade
- 2 tsp. stone-ground mustard
- 1 tsp. prepared horseradish

In a small bowl, combine marmalade, mustard and horseradish; mix well. Refrigerate for 1 hour before serving with grilled shrimp.

SHRIMP COCKTAIL DIP

Makes about 1¾ cups
- 1 C. light mayonnaise
- ½ to ¾ C. ketchup
- 1 to 1½ T. prepared horseradish

In a small bowl, combine mayonnaise, ketchup and horseradish; mix well. Serve with grilled shrimp.

TOMATO-BLACK OLIVE RELISH

Garnishes 4 servings
- ½ C. chopped black olives
- ½ C. chopped tomatoes
- ¼ C. balsamic vinaigrette dressing

In a small bowl, stir together olives, tomatoes and dressing. Let stand for 20 minutes to blend flavors before serving.

CUCUMBER-MELON SALSA

Garnishes 4 servings
- 1 C. peeled, diced cantaloupe
- ½ C. seeded, diced cucumber
- 2 T. minced fresh basil
- 1 T. minced green onion
- 1 T. honey
- 1 T. white wine vinegar
- 1 tsp. olive oil
- ½ tsp. coarse salt

In a medium bowl, combine cantaloupe, cucumber, basil, onion, honey, vinegar, oil and salt; mix well. Cover and chill for at least 30 minutes before serving with grilled shrimp.

Dip grilled shrimp into one of these flavorful sauces to add flair. Garnish grilled shrimp with a delicious relish or salsa.

PEAR-PINEAPPLE-MANGO SALSA

Garnishes 4 to 6 servings

1 pear, cored and cubed
1 C. cubed fresh pineapple
1 mango, peeled and cubed
2 T. lime juice
1 tsp. ground allspice

In a medium bowl, combine pear, pineapple, mango, lime juice and allspice; toss to combine. Let stand for at least 15 minutes to blend flavors before serving with grilled shrimp.

GRILLED SHRIMP PIZZA

Makes 8 servings

Juice from ½ fresh lime
Juice from ½ fresh orange
1 T. honey
3 T. olive oil, divided
2 cloves garlic, minced
1 tsp. soy sauce
¼ tsp. black pepper
¼ C. chopped fresh cilantro
1 lb. large raw shrimp, peeled, deveined
   and rinsed
1 red and/or yellow bell pepper, quartered
1 small zucchini, cut lengthwise into ½"
   thick slices
1 lb. fresh pizza dough or frozen
   dough, thawed
1 (8 oz.) can pineapple chunks
2 C. shredded Monterey Jack cheese, divided

In a medium bowl, combine lime juice, orange juice, honey, 2 tablespoons oil, garlic, soy sauce, black pepper and cilantro; mix well. Divide mixture between two large resealable plastic bags. Add shrimp to one bag; add bell pepper and zucchini to other bag; seal and turn to coat food. Refrigerate bags to marinate shrimp and vegetables for 15 minutes.

To cook, lightly oil the grate and preheat grill to medium heat. Remove food and discard marinades. Thread shrimp on metal or soaked wooden skewers and grill for 5 to 8 minutes or until shrimp turn pink, flipping several times. Grill vegetables for 6 to 8 minutes or until tender-crisp; remove from grill and dice. Remove shrimp from skewers. To assemble pizza, flatten dough to a 12" to 14" round, about ¼" thick. Brush dough with remaining 1 tablespoon oil. Place dough on the grate, oiled side down; cover grill. Cook for 1 to 2 minutes or until grill marks appear on bottom. Turn crust over with tongs or large spatula. Layer crust with half the cheese, grilled shrimp and vegetables; top with remaining cheese and pineapple. Cover grill and cook 3 to 4 minutes or until cheese melts and crust is brown. Check often and rotate as needed. Slide pizza onto a baking sheet to serve.

SCALLOPS

Scallops are delicate and cook very quickly on the grill, so take care not to overcook them or they can become rubbery. The grates on your grill must be very clean to prevent sticking. Lightly oiling both the grates and the scallops can prevent this problem. For the best flavor when purchasing fresh scallops, look for a "dry" label that means they were not treated with preservatives.

PERFECTLY GRILLED SCALLOPS

Makes 4 servings

1 lb. sea scallops, approximately 1" thick*
2 T. olive oil
Coarse salt to taste
Coarsely ground black pepper to taste

Rinse scallops in cool water and pat dry thoroughly with paper towels, pressing down gently to remove moisture. Allow scallops to stand on paper towels for 10 minutes. Place scallops in a medium bowl and drizzle with oil; toss well to coat.

To cook, lightly oil the cleaned grate and preheat grill to medium-high heat. Thread approximately six scallops horizontally on each metal or soaked wooden skewer. Season with salt and black pepper. Place skewers on the grate directly over heat and cook for 1 to 2 minutes or until golden brown grill marks appear. Turn once and cook 1 to 2 minutes longer or until just cooked through. Remove from the grill and let stand for 2 to 3 minutes before serving. Slide scallops off skewers and serve warm.

* If frozen, thaw completely and allow scallops to warm up to room temperature. Rinse and then pat dry several times. If scallops are big or thick, slice them in half horizontally before cooking.

BACON-WRAPPED SCALLOPS

Makes 4 servings

16 to 20 sea scallops (about 1½ lbs.)
¼ C. lemon juice
1 tsp. cayenne pepper or to taste
¼ tsp. garlic powder
8 to 10 strips bacon
1 lemon, cut into wedges

Rinse scallops and pat them dry with paper towels. In a large resealable plastic bag, combine lemon juice, cayenne pepper and garlic powder; mix well. Add scallops to bag, seal and turn to coat. Let scallops rest in marinade at room temperature for 10 minutes.

Meanwhile, lightly oil the cleaned grate and preheat grill to medium heat. Cut bacon slices in half, crosswise. In a large skillet over medium heat, cook bacon until partially cooked but not crisp. Drain on paper towels. Remove scallops and discard marinade. Wrap one piece of bacon around each scallop and thread on metal or soaked wooden skewers alternately with lemon wedges. Place skewers on the grate directly over heat, cover grill and cook for 8 to 12 minutes or until scallops are opaque, turning occasionally.

Wrap uncooked, peeled and deveined jumbo shrimp in bacon and add to skewers with scallops, if desired. Turn up the flavor on scallops when you wrap them in other foods before grilling.

VEGETABLES

BASIC COOKING TIPS

There's more to grilling than just meat! Vegetables are easy to grill and benefit from light marinating, glazing or basting. Use a grill basket to keep cut food from slipping through the grates or thread the pieces on skewers. Grilling in foil keeps moisture in food and saves on clean-up.

Use the following chart to determine the approximate temperature to heat your grill to match the heat level indicated by the recipe. For accuracy, use a thermometer to measure the temperature inside the grill.

	Grill Temperature
High heat	400°
Medium-high heat	375°
Medium heat	350°
Medium-low heat	325°
Low heat	300°

BELL PEPPERS

To grill whole, halved or quartered bell peppers, spray grate with nonstick cooking spray or brush peppers with oil; preheat grill to high heat. Remove seeds and membranes from halved or quartered peppers. Place peppers directly on grate. Grill approximately 5 minutes on each side, turning until skin is dark and charred on all sides. Remove from grill and place in a paper bag, closing tightly; let stand 10 to 15 minutes. Remove from bag and peel away charred skin.

    Variation: You can also serve peppers with the skin left intact. To do this, grill peppers until the skin has reached a slight golden brown color on each side. This method will produce flavors completely different from grilled peppers with the skins removed.

To grill filled bell peppers, remove tops from peppers about ½" from the stem; reserve. Remove seeds and membranes from peppers. Spoon filling into peppers; replace tops, securing with toothpicks. Preheat grill to medium heat. Place peppers on grate, top sides up, and cook 12 to 15 minutes or until peppers are soft but still hold their shape.

To grill filled bell peppers in foil, coat heavy-duty aluminum foil with nonstick cooking spray. Preheat grill to medium heat. Cut peppers in half, remove seeds and membranes and stuff each with filling. Place peppers on foil, folding foil over and sealing edges, allowing space inside for air circulation. Close grill lid for 15 to 20 minutes until peppers are tender.

To grill bell peppers on skewers, cut peppers into 1" pieces and thread onto skewers*. Coat peppers with oil or marinade and grill for about 10 minutes on a preheated hot grill, turning occasionally, until edges are browned.

* If using wooden skewers, be sure to soak in water at least 30 minutes before using to prevent burning.

SWEET GRILLED PEPPERS

Makes 4 servings

1 T. Dijon mustard
2 T. minced red onion
¼ C. red wine vinegar
4 cloves garlic, minced
Black pepper to taste
2 large red bell peppers, quartered, seeds and membranes removed
2 large green bell peppers, quartered, seeds and membranes removed

Oil grate; preheat grill to medium heat. In a small bowl, combine mustard, onion, vinegar, garlic and black pepper. Place peppers on the grill and brush with mustard mixture. Cook until lightly browned, turning occasionally and brushing with marinade; peppers should be slightly soft. Serve hot or cold with remaining marinade.

MARINATED GRILLED PEPPERS

Makes 4 servings

¾ C. chopped fresh cilantro
¼ C. white or red wine vinegar
⅓ C. olive oil
1½ tsp. finely grated lime peel
3 T. lime juice
¾ tsp. salt
¼ tsp. sugar
¼ tsp. hot pepper sauce
¼ tsp. black pepper
1½ lbs. sweet bell peppers, quartered, seeds and membranes removed

In a small bowl, whisk together cilantro, vinegar, oil, lime peel, lime juice, salt, sugar, pepper sauce and black pepper. Pour into a resealable plastic bag; add peppers. Seal bag and turn to coat vegetables. Refrigerate, turning occasionally, up to 4 hours. Remove peppers from bag and reserve marinade. Oil grate and preheat grill to medium heat. Grill vegetables on grate until browned and slightly soft, turning and brushing occasionally with marinade.

HERB GRILLED VEGETABLES

Makes 4 servings

⅓ C. olive oil
3 T. lemon juice
2 tsp. basil, crushed, dried
2 tsp. dried thyme
1½ tsp. salt
¼ tsp. black pepper
1½ lbs. sweet bell peppers, quartered, seeds and membranes removed

In a small bowl, whisk together oil, lemon juice, basil, thyme, salt and black pepper. Pour into a resealable plastic bag; add bell peppers. Seal bag and turn to coat well. Refrigerate, turning occasionally, for up to 4 hours. Oil grate. Reserving marinade, place peppers directly on preheated, medium-hot grill. Turn and brush vegetables occasionally with marinade. Remove from grill when browned and slightly softened.

Bell Peppers

VEGETABLES

ASIAN GRILLED PEPPERS

Makes 4 servings

1 large shallot, finely minced
3½ T. balsamic vinegar
2 T. soy sauce
1½ tsp. sesame oil
1 tsp. Dijon mustard
1 clove garlic, minced
¼ tsp. sugar
⅛ tsp. hot pepper sauce
1½ lbs. sweet bell peppers, quartered, seeds and membranes removed

In a small bowl, whisk together shallot, vinegar, soy sauce, oil, mustard, garlic, sugar and hot pepper sauce. Oil grate and preheat grill to medium or medium-high heat. Do not marinate bell peppers, but brush with mixture just before grilling and once when turning, halfway through cooking time. Grill until browned and slightly soft.

GRILLED RED PEPPERS WITH MOZZARELLA

Makes 4 to 6 servings

1 small loaf crusty Italian bread
4 T. olive oil, divided
3 sweet red bell peppers
1 C. fresh mozzarella cheese, cut into small cubes
1½ tsp. dried basil
1 clove garlic, finely chopped
Salt to taste
Black pepper to taste

Preheat grill to medium heat. Thinly slice bread, removing crusts, and cut into enough ½" cubes to make 2 cups. In a skillet, sauté bread in 3 tablespoons oil until golden; drain on paper towels. Cut tops off bell peppers about ½" from the stem and reserve. Carefully remove seeds and membranes. In a small bowl, combine bread cubes, cheese, basil, garlic and remaining 1 tablespoon oil. Mix well, adding salt and black pepper. Stuff peppers with mixture and grill as directed for grilling filled bell peppers on page 101.

Bell peppers lend themselves easily to stuffing. Without much preparation, you can make a delicious side dish consisting of a variety of flavors, all warmed within the pepper. And the bonus? You get to eat the "bowl!"

BACON & CORN STUFFED PEPPERS

Makes 4 servings

2 C. frozen corn, thawed
⅓ C. salsa
6 green onions, chopped
1 medium green bell pepper, halved, seeds and membranes removed
1 medium red bell pepper, halved, seeds and membranes removed
¼ C. shredded mozzarella cheese
2 bacon strips, cooked and crumbled
Additional salsa, optional

Preheat grill to medium heat. In a large bowl, combine corn, salsa and onions; spoon mixture into bell pepper halves. Grill as directed for grilling filled bell peppers in foil on page 101. Sprinkle with cheese and bacon. Return to grill for 3 to 5 minutes or until cheese is melted. Serve with additional salsa, if desired.

BLACK BEAN & RICE STUFFED PEPPERS

Makes 6 servings

1 (15 oz.) can black beans, drained and rinsed
¾ C. cooked white rice
4 medium green onions, sliced
¼ C. chopped fresh cilantro
2 T. vegetable oil
2 T. lime juice
1 clove garlic, finely chopped
¼ tsp. salt
3 large bell peppers, cut in half lengthwise, seeds and membranes removed
1 roma tomato, diced

Preheat grill to medium heat. Mix beans, rice, onions, cilantro, oil, lime juice, garlic and salt. Stuff bell pepper halves with mixture and grill as directed for grilling filled bell peppers in foil on page 101. Carefully open foil packets and sprinkle with tomato.

GRILLED THREE-PEPPER SALAD

Makes 4 to 6 servings

1 each large green, red and yellow bell pepper, seeded and cut into 1" pieces
½ large red onion, halved and thinly sliced
½ lb. mozzarella cheese, cut into bite-size cubes
1 (2.25 oz.) can pitted ripe olives, drained and halved
⅓ C. olive oil
3 T. red wine vinegar
1 T. lemon juice
1 T. Dijon mustard
½ tsp. dried basil
¼ tsp. cayenne pepper
¼ tsp. garlic powder

Brush grate with oil and preheat grill to medium heat. Thread bell peppers onto skewers* and grill for 10 to 12 minutes or until edges are brown. Remove from skewers and place in a large bowl. Add onion, cheese and olives; toss gently. Cover and refrigerate. For vinaigrette, in a jar with a tight-fitting lid, combine oil, vinegar, lemon juice, mustard, basil, cayenne pepper and garlic powder; shake well. Pour over bell pepper mixture just before serving; toss to coat.

* If using wooden skewers, be sure to soak in water at least 30 minutes before using to prevent burning.

Bell Peppers

VEGETABLES

BALSAMIC-HERB RATATOUILLE

Makes 6 servings

5 T. balsamic vinegar, divided
2 T. olive oil
1 medium eggplant
1 small onion, peeled and quartered
2 medium yellow or red bell peppers, seeded and cut into 1" pieces
12 whole, fresh mushrooms
2 small zucchini, halved lengthwise
½ pint cherry tomatoes
4 cloves garlic, minced
1 tsp. dried oregano
1 tsp. dried thyme
1 tsp. Dijon mustard
½ tsp. black pepper
⅓ C. fresh basil, chopped

Oil grate and preheat grill to medium heat. Spray casserole dish with nonstick cooking spray; set aside. In a small bowl, combine 2 tablespoons vinegar and oil; set aside for basting. Slice eggplant into ½" thick rounds. Thread onion onto skewers*. Baste eggplant and onion with vinegar-oil mixture. Place skewers and eggplant on grate, close lid and grill about 10 minutes or until tender, basting and turning occasionally. Slice eggplant into bite-size pieces. Add onion and eggplant to casserole dish; keep warm. Thread bell peppers and mushrooms onto skewers. Baste mushrooms, peppers and cut sides of zucchini with vinegar-oil mixture. Add skewers and zucchini to grate and cook 10 to 15 minutes until tender and edges of peppers are browned, basting and turning once. Cut zucchini into ½" slices. Add peppers, mushrooms and zucchini to casserole dish; keep warm. Thread tomatoes onto skewers and grill 5 minutes or until skin is blistered, basting and turning once. Add to casserole dish; keep warm. In a small bowl, whisk together garlic, remaining 3 tablespoons vinegar, oregano, thyme, mustard and black pepper. Stir into vegetables and sprinkle with basil.

* If using wooden skewers, be sure to soak in water at least 30 minutes before using to prevent burning.

MUSHROOMS

To grill large, flat mushrooms (such as Portobello mushrooms), brush both sides with olive oil and place on a preheated hot grill for about 4 minutes on each side. Or, thickly slice the mushrooms and lay them perpendicular to the grate. If stuffing mushrooms, brush the tops with olive oil and place about ½ tablespoon butter inside each. Place on a preheated hot grill, top side down, for about 4 minutes. Add stuffing and return to grill, top side down, for an additional 4 minutes.

To grill small mushroom caps (such as button mushrooms), spray a grill basket or heavy-duty aluminum foil with nonstick cooking spray. Toss the mushrooms in olive oil and place in basket. Preheat grill to medium heat. Grill mushrooms until tender. If stuffing mushrooms, remove stems. Fill mushroom caps with stuffing and place on preheated medium-hot grill, in a disposable foil pan, on heavy-duty aluminum foil sprayed with nonstick cooking spray or in a grill basket. Grill until filling is warm and mushrooms are tender.

To grill mushrooms for kebabs, thread similar mushrooms on the same skewer*. If using multiple varieties or sizes, put each type or size on its own skewer. Cooking times will vary by type and size. Grill over medium heat until mushrooms are tender.

To sauté mushrooms, use a disposable foil pan or heavy-duty aluminum foil, crimping the sides to make a shallow pan; spray with nonstick cooking spray. Add a single layer of mushrooms and cook until mushrooms become browned on the bottom. Flip and cook until other side is browned.

* If using wooden skewers, be sure to soak in water at least 30 minutes before using to prevent burning.

Mushrooms come in many shapes and sizes, all of them perfect for grilling. They absorb marinades and sauces like meat and are very versatile on the grill. Whether you grill them directly on the grate, in a grill basket, stuffed or skewered, there's a mushroom for your purpose.

TARRAGON-MARINATED MUSHROOMS

Makes about 1¼ cups

½ C. olive oil
1/3 C. tarragon vinegar
1 clove garlic, crushed
1 medium onion, sliced thin
Dash hot sauce
1 lb. fresh mushrooms, cut into bite-size
  pieces, if needed

In a deep, non-metal bowl, whisk together oil, vinegar, garlic, onion, hot sauce and 1 tablespoon water. Add mushrooms and marinate in the refrigerator at least 8 hours. Drain and grill as directed on page 107.

SIMPLE HERB MUSHROOMS

Makes about 2 cups

1½ lbs. fresh mushrooms, stems removed
3 T. olive oil
1 tsp. dried thyme
1 tsp. salt
3 T. lemon juice
1 T. minced garlic
½ tsp. black pepper
3 T. dried parsley
⅛ tsp. onion powder

In a large bowl, whisk together oil, thyme, salt, lemon juice, garlic, black pepper, parsley and onion powder. Add mushrooms, tossing to coat. Chill mushrooms in marinade overnight. Grill as directed on page 107.

SIMPLE MARINATED MUSHROOMS

Makes 4 servings

1 lb. fresh mushrooms, stems removed
  and reserved
1/3 C. red wine vinegar
2½ T. olive oil
Salt to taste
Black pepper to taste
1 clove garlic, crushed
Grated Parmesan cheese

Cut stems into thick slices and place slices and caps in a resealable plastic bag. In a small bowl, combine vinegar, oil, salt, black pepper and garlic. Add marinade to mushrooms. Seal bag. Refrigerate at least 15 minutes, but no longer than 2 hours. Preheat grill to medium heat. Place mushrooms and marinade on heavy-duty aluminum foil. Fold foil around mushrooms and seal edges, creating a packet. Place packet on the grill for about 12 to 16 minutes, turning every few minutes. Remove foil packet from grill and open carefully. Remove mushrooms and sprinkle with Parmesan cheese.

SAVORY MUSHROOMS IN MARINADE

Makes 4 servings

2½ C. canola oil
1 C. white vinegar
1 bunch chives, chopped
1 bunch green onions, finely chopped
2½ T. sugar
1½ T. salt
1 T. lemon juice
1 T. finely minced garlic
2 tsp. Worcestershire sauce
2 tsp. bottled browning sauce
⅛ tsp. prepared yellow mustard
1 lb. fresh mushrooms, stems removed

In a deep bowl, whisk together oil, vinegar, chives, onions, sugar, salt, lemon juice, garlic, Worcestershire sauce, browning sauce and mustard. Add mushrooms; cover and marinate 4 hours or overnight in the refrigerator. Grill as directed on page 107.

ITALIAN STUFFED MUSHROOMS

Makes about 24 appetizers

1 lb. medium-sized fresh mushrooms
2 T. butter
¼ C. chopped green onion
¼ C. chopped red bell pepper
1½ C. soft bread crumbs
2 tsp. Italian seasoning
¼ tsp. salt
¼ tsp. black pepper
Grated Parmesan cheese

Preheat grill to medium heat. Remove stems from mushroom caps. Finely chop enough stems to measure ⅓ cup; reserve. In a 10" skillet over medium-high heat, melt butter. Cook chopped mushroom stems, onion and bell pepper in butter about 3 minutes, stirring frequently, until onions are softened; remove from heat. Stir in bread crumbs, Italian seasoning, salt and black pepper. Fill mushroom caps and sprinkle with cheese. Grill mushrooms, stuffing side up, until tender and filling is hot.

Turn the humble mushroom into the star of your next party with the help of these fabulous recipes.

BLUE CHEESE STUFFED MUSHROOMS

Makes about 10 to 12 appetizers

½ lb. fresh mushrooms, stems removed
4 oz. blue cheese

Lightly oil grate and preheat grill to high heat. Fill mushroom caps with crumbled blue cheese. Grill as directed for stuffing small mushroom caps on page 107.

VEGETABLE-STUFFED MUSHROOMS

Makes 16 to 20 appetizers

16 to 20 fresh small mushrooms
1 small zucchini, shredded
2 T. sliced green onion
⅓ C. grated Parmesan cheese

Preheat grill to medium-high heat. Remove and chop mushroom stems. In a medium saucepan, combine stems, zucchini, onion and 1 tablespoon water. Cook and stir over medium heat until vegetables are tender; drain. Stir in Parmesan cheese. Divide mixture among mushroom caps. Grill mushrooms, stuffing side up, until tender and filling is hot.

CRAB-STUFFED MUSHROOMS

Makes 12 appetizers

12 fresh small mushrooms
1 (8 oz.) pkg. cream cheese, softened
1 cluster of steamed crab meat, cut into small pieces
3 cloves garlic, chopped
4 oz. shredded mozzarella cheese
4 oz. Asiago cheese

Preheat grill to medium heat. Remove and chop mushroom stems. In a large bowl, combine cream cheese, crab meat, garlic and stems. Stuff mushrooms with cream cheese mixture. In a small bowl, combine mozzarella and Asiago cheeses; dip stuffed side of each mushroom into the mixture. Place mushrooms, stuffing side up, on a disposable foil pan or heavy-duty aluminum foil which has been sprayed with nonstick cooking spray. Grill with lid closed until cheese is melted.

CHEESY MUSHROOMS

Makes 12 appetizers

12 fresh small mushrooms
1 T. olive oil
1 T. minced garlic
1 (8 oz.) pkg. cream cheese, softened
¼ C. grated Parmesan cheese
¼ tsp. black pepper
¼ tsp. onion powder
¼ tsp. cayenne pepper

Preheat grill to medium heat. Lightly grease a disposable foil pan. Remove, chop and mince mushroom stems. Heat oil in large skillet over medium heat. Add garlic and stems. Cook until soft; set aside. Once cooled, stir in cream cheese, Parmesan cheese, black pepper, onion powder and cayenne pepper. Fill mushroom caps and arrange, stuffing side up, on prepared pan. Grill until hot.

FOUR-CHEESE MUSHROOMS

Makes 12 appetizers

12 fresh small mushrooms
1 T. olive oil
1 T. minced onion
½ tsp. minced garlic
½ tsp. dried basil
¼ C. white wine
½ C. shredded provolone cheese
½ C. shredded mozzarella cheese
¼ C. grated Parmesan cheese
¼ C. grated Romano cheese

Remove, chop and mince mushroom stems; set aside. Heat oil in a large skillet over medium heat. Add onion, garlic and stems. Cook until soft, about 5 minutes. Add basil and wine. Simmer until liquid is nearly absorbed, about 7 minutes. Cool slightly. Stir in provolone, mozzarella, Parmesan and Romano cheeses. Preheat grill to medium heat. Place mushrooms in a lightly greased disposable foil pan. Fill caps with cheese mixture and grill, stuffing side up, until hot.

SPINACH-STUFFED PORTOBELLO MUSHROOMS

Makes 4 servings

10 to 12 oz. baby spinach
Olive oil
½ C. chopped onion
2 cloves garlic, minced
1 C. chopped fresh tomatoes
¼ C. chopped sun-dried tomatoes
¼ C. diced black olives
Salt to taste
Black pepper to taste
¼ C. bread crumbs
4 portobello mushrooms

Place spinach in a large saucepan and cook 2 minutes until wilted, stirring constantly. Remove from heat and drain. Add oil, onion and garlic to pan. Cook until tender. Add fresh and dried tomatoes, olives, salt and black pepper. Cook 2 to 3 minutes. Preheat grill to medium heat. Remove mushroom stems and discard. Brush tops of mushrooms with oil and season with salt and black pepper. Place on grill, top side down, and cook for 5 to 6 minutes. Remove from grill. Stuff mushrooms with spinach mixture. In a small bowl, combine bread crumbs with salt and black pepper. Sprinkle bread crumbs over spinach mixture. Place mushrooms on grill, stuffing side up, for an additional 5 to 10 minutes.

ROASTED RED PEPPER PORTOBELLOS

Makes 4 servings

4 portobello mushrooms, stems removed
2 tsp. balsamic vinegar
2 C. diced water-packed roasted red peppers
1 tsp. minced garlic
1 T. chopped fresh basil
1 T. olive oil
¼ tsp. salt
¼ tsp. black pepper
1 oz. Parmesan cheese, thinly sliced

Preheat grill to medium-high heat. Place mushrooms in a disposable foil pan and rub bottoms of each mushroom with ½ teaspoon vinegar; lightly coat with cooking spray. Place mushrooms on grill, top side up, with grill lid closed, for about 4 minutes. Flip mushrooms and cook an additional 4 to 5 minutes. Remove to cool. Meanwhile, in a medium bowl, combine red pepper, garlic, basil, oil, salt and black pepper. Cut cooled mushrooms into quarters and top each with about 2 tablespoons of red pepper mixture and sliced cheese.

GOAT CHEESE PORTOBELLOS

Makes 4 servings

4 portobello mushrooms
¼ C. olive oil
2 cloves garlic, minced
6 oz. crumbled goat cheese
2 oz. prosciutto or thinly sliced
    ham, chopped
¼ C. chopped fresh basil

Remove stems and gently scrape gills from undersides of mushrooms; discard stems and gills. In a small bowl, combine oil and garlic; brush on mushroom caps. In a medium bowl, combine cheese, prosciutto and basil; set aside. Grill mushrooms, top side up, on covered grill over medium heat for 4 minutes. Turn mushrooms over; fill caps with cheese mixture. Cover and grill 3 to 4 minutes longer until cheese mixture is warm.

MUSHROOM & BACON BITES

Makes 4 to 6 servings

24 medium fresh mushrooms
12 strips bacon, halved
1 C. barbeque sauce

Preheat grill to medium heat. Wrap each mushroom with a strip of bacon; secure with a toothpick. Thread onto skewers*; brush with barbeque sauce. Grill, uncovered, over indirect heat for 10 to 15 minutes or until bacon is crisp and mushrooms are tender, turning and basting occasionally with remaining barbecue sauce.

* If using wooden skewers, be sure to soak in water at least 30 minutes before using to prevent burning.

MUSHROOM KEBABS

Makes about 4 servings

¾ C. fresh mushrooms
2 red bell peppers, seeded and cut into
    1" pieces
1 green bell pepper, seeded and cut into
    1" pieces
¼ C. olive oil
2 T. lemon juice
1 clove garlic, minced
2 tsp. chopped fresh thyme
1 tsp. chopped fresh rosemary
¼ tsp. salt
¼ tsp. black pepper

Brush grate with oil and preheat grill to medium heat. Thread mushrooms, red and green bell peppers alternately on skewers*. In a small bowl, mix oil, lemon juice, garlic, thyme, rosemary, salt and black pepper. Brush mushrooms and bell peppers with oil mixture and place kebabs on grill. Baste frequently with oil mixture during grilling. Cook about 4 to 6 minutes or until mushrooms are tender and thoroughly cooked.

* If using wooden skewers, be sure to soak in water at least 30 minutes before using to prevent burning.

PORTOBELLO SOUP

Makes 4 servings

¾ lb. portobello mushrooms
1 T. olive oil
2 T. minced shallots
1 clove garlic, minced
1 leek (white parts only), sliced
2 medium carrots, peeled and chopped
2 stalks celery, chopped
1 T. soy sauce
4 C. chicken or vegetable broth
Salt to taste
Black pepper to taste

Grill mushrooms as directed on page 107. Dice mushrooms and set aside. In a large saucepan, heat oil over medium-high heat. Add shallots and garlic; cook until softened, about 2 minutes, stirring frequently. Add leek, carrots and celery. Cook stirring frequently, until vegetables start to soften, about 5 minutes. Add soy sauce and broth. Bring to a boil on high heat. Cover and reduce heat to low. Simmer 15 minutes. Season with salt and black pepper. Add mushrooms and heat through.

MINI MUSHROOM MAC 'N' CHEESE

Makes 4 servings

2 C. (4 oz.) uncooked cavatappi (or other spiral, tube-shaped pasta)
1 lb. assorted mushrooms, cut into ½" pieces
1 T. olive oil
¼ C. butter
¼ C. flour
½ tsp. salt
2 C. milk
6 oz. fresh goat cheese
½ C. shredded mozzarella cheese
2 T. minced fresh rosemary
1 T. minced fresh thyme

Preheat grill to medium heat. Cook pasta according to package directions. Grill mushrooms in a disposable foil pan with oil until mushrooms brown on one side. Turn mushrooms and grill until the other side is brown. In a large saucepan, melt butter and stir in flour. Cook to lightly toast flour. Stir in salt and whisk in milk. Bring to a low boil over medium-high heat, stirring occasionally to slightly thicken sauce, about 5 minutes. Remove sauce from heat, add goat cheese, mozzarella cheese, rosemary and thyme; stir until cheeses melt. Stir in mushrooms and pasta and place into a 4- to 6-cup foil pan that has been sprayed with nonstick cooking spray. Cover pan with aluminum foil and place on grill; close lid. Bake until cheese bubbles around edges, about 15 to 20 minutes. Remove from grill and let rest about 5 minutes. Serve warm.

POTATOES

For whole or halved potatoes, pierce skin with a fork and place on a medium to hot grill. Close lid and bake about 1 hour or until easily pierced with a fork, turning halfway through baking time.

Variation: Wrap each potato in heavy-duty aluminum foil, adding oil and seasonings before sealing, if desired.

For potato wedges, cut lengthwise into wedges. Toss with oil and seasonings. Preheat grill to low heat. Place cut side down on grate. Close lid and cook until deep golden brown, about 4 to 6 minutes on each side.*

For potato slices, slice about ¼" thick, toss with oil and seasonings and place in a single layer on a grill heated to medium heat. Close lid and turn potatoes when browned. Repeat on other side until tender.*

For potato fries, slice into ½ x ½" sticks the length of the potato. Carefully place in a resealable bag; add oil and seasonings, turning to coat well. Preheat grill to medium heat. Place in a single layer on grill and grill until browned on all sides.*

For potato chips, slice into very thin slices. Toss with oil and seasonings. Place in a single layer on grill heated to medium until browned; carefully turn and grill until browned on other side.*

For potatoes in aluminum foil packet, cut potatoes into cubes. Toss with oil and seasonings and place in an even layer on heavy-duty aluminum foil large enough to wrap completely around the potatoes, leaving enough space inside for air to circulate. Place on a grill heated to medium-low and close lid for about 40 minutes.

* Variation: To cut down on grilling time, cut potatoes as desired. Pre-cook by simmering in water on stove until nearly tender. Drain well. Coat with oil. Leaving the grill uncovered, grill potatoes on both sides until golden brown. Season as desired.

Potatoes have been a versatile staple in the kitchen for centuries, making them a popular side dish. Take your potatoes out of the kitchen and onto the grill.

OLIVE OIL & FRESH HERBS

Seasons 1 pound of potatoes

2 to 3 T. olive oil
Salt to taste
Black pepper to taste
2 to 3 tsp. chopped fresh rosemary, thyme
    or sage

Toss potatoes with enough oil to coat well. Season with salt, black pepper and rosemary, thyme or sage. Grill to desired doneness.

LIME-THYME SEASONING

Seasons 1 pound of potatoes

¼ C. margarine, melted
1 T. lime juice
1 tsp. finely grated lime peel
1 tsp. dried thyme
¼ C. grated Romano cheese
½ tsp. salt
¼ tsp. paprika

In a large bowl, combine margarine, lime juice, lime peel and thyme. Add potatoes; toss to coat. In a small bowl, combine cheese, salt and paprika; sprinkle over potatoes. Grill to desired doneness.

SEASONED GARLIC BUTTER GLAZE

Seasons 1 pound of potatoes

¼ C. butter, melted
2 cloves garlic, crushed
1 T. seasoned salt
½ tsp. black pepper

Combine butter, garlic, seasoned salt and black pepper; coat potatoes. Grill to desired doneness.

Use the seasoning mixes above to flavor a pound of potatoes (about 12 to 14 baby potatoes, 6 medium potatoes or 2 large potatoes) before they go on the grill. Slice potatoes as desired, add seasoning or glaze of your choice and grill as directed on page 115.

CREAMY ITALIAN MIX

Seasons 1 pound of potatoes
½ C. bottled Italian dressing
½ C. mayonnaise
1 tsp. salt
½ tsp. black pepper

Combine dressing, mayonnaise, salt and black pepper; coat potatoes. Grill to desired doneness.

DRY SPICE RUB

Seasons 1 pound of potatoes
2 to 3 T. olive oil
½ tsp. ground cumin
½ tsp. ground coriander
½ tsp. paprika
½ tsp. chili powder
½ tsp. ground allspice
½ tsp. black pepper
½ tsp. dried thyme
1½ tsp. salt
Pinch sugar

Coat potatoes with olive oil. Combine cumin, coriander, paprika, chili powder, allspice, black pepper, thyme, salt and sugar. Sprinkle dry rub over all cut edges of potatoes. Grill to desired doneness.

ROASTED RED PEPPER & HERB SAUCE

Makes about 1½ cups
1 (12 oz.) jar roasted red peppers, drained
1 T. balsamic vinegar
½ tsp. Italian seasoning
¼ tsp. garlic powder
Salt to taste

In a medium bowl, combine peppers, vinegar, Italian seasoning and garlic powder. Transfer mixture to a blender or food processor and process until smooth. Season with salt and serve with hot grilled potatoes.

Any of these sauces can be used as a dip with any grilled potatoes.

CREAMY HORSERADISH SAUCE

Makes about 1¼ cups

3 T. prepared horseradish
1 (8 oz.) container sour cream
Salt to taste

Combine horseradish and sour cream. Season with salt and serve with hot grilled potatoes.

CARAMELIZED ONION & CHIVE DIPPING SAUCE

Makes about 1½ cups

1 T. olive oil
1 medium onion, quartered and thinly sliced
1 C. fat-free Greek yogurt
¼ C. sliced fresh chives
2 T. minced fresh rosemary
Salt to taste
Black pepper to taste

In a medium skillet, heat oil. Add onion and cook over low heat for 20 minutes, stirring frequently; let cool. Puree onion and yogurt in a blender or food processor until smooth. Add chives and rosemary; pulse until finely chopped. Season with salt and black pepper. Serve with hot grilled potatoes.

BBQ SAUCE

Makes about 1¼ cups

¾ C. bottled chili sauce
¼ C. steak sauce
1 T. Worcestershire sauce
1 T. red wine vinegar
1 T. dry mustard

In a medium bowl, combine chili sauce, steak sauce, Worcestershire sauce, vinegar and mustard. Serve with hot grilled potatoes.

SPICY POTATO SKINS

Makes about 4 servings

2 large potatoes (about 1 lb.)
2 T. olive oil
½ tsp. salt
¼ tsp. black pepper
¾ tsp. chili powder
¾ tsp. curry powder
¾ tsp. ground coriander

Grill whole potatoes as directed on page 115. Slice potatoes in half lengthwise and cool for about 10 minutes. Remove pulp, leaving a shell about ¼" thick. Brush each potato with oil. Combine salt, black pepper, chili powder, curry powder and coriander; sprinkle over potatoes. Grill until crispy and brown.

LOADED POTATO SKINS

Makes about 4 servings

2 large potatoes (about 1 lb.), each cut
    lengthwise into 4 wedges
2 T. butter, melted
2 T. picante sauce
¼ C. shredded Cheddar cheese
1½ T. bacon bits, divided
¼ C. chopped tomatoes
2 T. chopped green onion
3 T. mayonnaise
2 T. sour cream
1 T. ranch dressing
¼ tsp. garlic powder

Preheat grill to medium-hot heat. Grill potatoes as directed on page 115. Remove pulp from potatoes, leaving a ¼" thick shell. Brush with butter. Divide picante sauce, cheese and 1 tablespoon bacon bits evenly among skins. Grill potatoes with lid open, skin side down, 4 to 6 minutes or until golden brown. Close lid and cook 2 to 3 minutes longer. Remove from grill and sprinkle with tomatoes and onion. In a small bowl, combine mayonnaise, sour cream, dressing, garlic powder and remaining ½ tablespoon bacon bits. Serve with potatoes.

BASIC GRILLED POTATO PACKETS

Makes 4 to 6 servings

1½ to 2 lbs. potatoes, peeled and
    thinly sliced
Salt and black pepper to taste
2 T. butter or olive oil

Preheat grill to medium heat. Spray a sheet of heavy-duty aluminum foil with nonstick cooking spray. On center of aluminum foil, combine potatoes, salt and black pepper. Dot with butter or drizzle with oil. Fold foil around potatoes, securely sealing all edges to make a packet. Grill with lid closed, 20 to 30 minutes or until tender, carefully flipping once halfway through cooking time.

Foil packets are a great way to make potatoes quickly and easily and without the hassle of clean-up. Kept wrapped, they will stay warm off the grill for 20 to 30 minutes. Caution: The steam from the packets will be very hot; open the packet carefully with tongs, allowing the steam to escape away from you.

CHEESY POTATOES WITH BACON

Makes 4 to 6 servings

1½ to 2 lbs. potatoes, peeled and
    thinly sliced
8 strips bacon, cooked and crumbled
1 large onion, chopped
1½ C. mozzarella cheese
½ C. grated Parmesan cheese
2 tsp. salt
1 tsp. black pepper
6 T. butter

Preheat grill to medium heat. Spray a large sheet of heavy-duty aluminum foil with nonstick cooking spray. On foil, combine potatoes, bacon and onion; sprinkle with mozzarella and Parmesan cheeses, salt and black pepper. Dot with butter. Fold foil, sealing all edges to make a packet. Grill over medium heat, with grill lid closed, 20 to 30 minutes or until tender.

LEMON-GARLIC POTATOES

Makes 4 to 6 servings

1½ to 2 lbs. potatoes, peeled and
    thinly sliced
10 cloves garlic, peeled
1¼ tsp. finely grated lemon peel
¾ tsp. salt
¼ tsp. black pepper
1½ T. olive oil

Preheat grill to medium heat. Spray a sheet of heavy-duty aluminum foil with nonstick cooking spray. On foil, combine potatoes, garlic, lemon peel, salt and black pepper. Drizzle with oil. Fold foil around potatoes, securely sealing all edges to make a packet. Grill over medium heat, with grill lid closed, 20 to 30 minutes or until tender, carefully flipping once halfway through cooking time.

CAMPFIRE POTATOES

Makes 4 to 6 servings

1½ to 2 lbs. potatoes, peeled and
    thinly sliced
1 onion, sliced
⅓ C. butter
⅓ C. shredded Cheddar cheese
2 T. minced fresh parsley
1 T. Worcestershire sauce
⅓ C. chicken broth
Salt and black pepper to taste

Preheat grill to medium heat. Spray a sheet of heavy-duty aluminum foil with nonstick cooking spray. On foil, combine potatoes and onion; dot with butter. In a small bowl, combine cheese, parsley, Worcestershire sauce, salt and pepper; add to potatoes. Partially fold foil around potatoes; add chicken broth. Secure foil around potatoes, sealing all edges to make a packet. Grill over medium heat, with grill lid closed, 20 to 30 minutes or until tender.

GRILLED POTATO SALAD

Makes about 6 servings

1½ lbs. potatoes (not small new potatoes)
¾ C. plus 2 T. olive oil, divided
Salt to taste
Black pepper to taste
2 tsp. Dijon mustard
¾ C. apple cider vinegar
1 T. finely chopped fresh rosemary
½ C. chopped black olives

Spray grate with nonstick cooking spray. Preheat grill to medium heat. Slice potatoes into ¼" thick slices. In a large bowl, combine 2 tablespoons of the oil, salt and black pepper. Add potatoes, tossing to coat. Place potato slices on the grate and grill 5 to 8 minutes per side. Meanwhile, in a small bowl, whisk together mustard, vinegar, remaining ¾ cup oil, salt and black pepper to make a vinaigrette. Stir in rosemary and olives. When potatoes are tender, transfer them back to the large bowl, cutting them into smaller pieces, if desired. Pour vinaigrette over potatoes and toss well while still warm. The potatoes will absorb the vinaigrette.

VEGETABLES

SWEET CORN

Grilling sweet corn in husks is an easy way to grill corn without it being noticeably grilled. The ears simply steam inside the outer layer. When grilling corn with this method, pull husks back from corn, keeping husks attached. Remove as much silk from the corn as possible; replace husks, covering kernels. Using kitchen twine, secure husks at tops. Place corn in a large bowl of cold water; let soak 30 to 60 minutes. Transfer corn to preheated medium-hot grill. Cook until husks are charred and the corn has steamed, about 15 minutes, turning to cook evenly. Remove from grill; discard husks.

Grilling sweet corn without husks provides the most obvious grilled effect by producing a more blackened ear of corn with a nutty, smoky flavor. When using this method to grill corn, completely remove and discard all husks and silk. Preheat grill to medium. Spray grate or ears of corn with nonstick cooking spray. Place corn directly on the grate and grill, with grill lid closed. Turn frequently, until cooked through, about 25 to 30 minutes. Watch closely—ears should be charred but not burned.

Grilling sweet corn in aluminum foil is another way to steam the corn. To grill corn using this method, simply preheat grill to medium-high heat. Place corn on a sheet of heavy-duty aluminum foil (approximately 18 x 24" for four ears of corn). Spread butter on corn and sprinkle with seasonings, if desired. Add a couple ice cubes to create extra moisture. Bring up foil sides and double fold top and ends to seal, leaving room for heat circulation. Grill with lid closed approximately 15 to 20 minutes, turning packet over once. Open foil carefully.

The smoky flavor that comes from sweet corn made on the grill can be a nice change of pace to traditional boiling methods. Whether you're looking for a hint of smokiness or a lot, one of the methods above should get your mind poppin' with ideas.

HERB BUTTER

Makes about ½ cup

½ C. butter, softened
2 tsp. minced fresh thyme
2 tsp. minced fresh oregano

Mix butter, thyme and oregano; chill before serving, if desired.

CAJUN BUTTER

Makes about ½ cup

½ C. butter, softened
1 tsp. garlic salt
¼ tsp. black pepper
¼ tsp. cayenne pepper
⅛ tsp. ground ginger
⅛ tsp. ground cloves

Mix butter, garlic salt, black pepper, cayenne pepper, ginger and cloves; chill, if desired.

CHIPOTLE-LIME BUTTER

Makes about ½ cup

½ C. butter, softened
1 tsp. finely grated lime peel
½ tsp. salt
⅛ to ¼ tsp. ground chipotle chile pepper
Dash of cayenne pepper

Mix butter, lime peel, salt, chile pepper and cayenne pepper; chill before serving, if desired.

Brush ears of sweet corn with flavored butter before grilling or serve it alongside warm, grilled sweet corn for a punch of flavor.

ITALIAN BUTTER

Makes about ½ cup

½ C. butter, softened
1 T. chopped fresh basil
1 T. chopped fresh oregano
1 tsp. finely chopped fresh garlic
½ tsp. salt

Mix butter, basil, oregano, garlic and salt; chill before serving, if desired.

CHIVE BUTTER

Makes about ½ cup

½ C. butter, softened
½ tsp. salt
¼ tsp. black pepper
2 tsp. chopped chives

Mix butter, salt, black pepper and chives; chill before serving, if desired.

DILL BUTTER

Makes about ½ cup

½ C. butter, softened
½ tsp. salt
¼ tsp. black pepper
1 tsp. dillweed

Mix butter, salt, black pepper and dillweed; chill before serving, if desired.

CORN CHOWDER

Makes 10 servings

4 ears sweet corn
3 strips bacon, minced
1 C. chopped onions
⅓ C. chopped green bell pepper
⅓ C. chopped red bell pepper
½ C. flour
5 C. chicken stock
1 lb. potatoes, cut into ½" pieces
1 bay leaf
1 C. heavy whipping cream
½ tsp. salt
½ tsp. Worcestershire sauce
¼ tsp. ground white pepper
¼ tsp. hot pepper sauce

Grill sweet corn as directed on page 122; allow to cool. Cut corn kernels from the cob with a sharp knife; set aside. Cook bacon over low heat until crisp. Add onions and cook 2 minutes or until transparent. Add green and red bell peppers and cook for 6 minutes, until peppers are tender. Add flour; stir and cook for 3 minutes. Gradually add chicken stock. Bring to a boil, stirring frequently. Add corn, potatoes and bay leaf; simmer 20 minutes. Add cream, salt, Worcestershire sauce, white pepper and hot pepper sauce. Simmer until heated.

Try cooking all the vegetables on the grill for this yummy chowder.

SWEET POTATOES

To grill whole sweet potatoes, pierce skin with a fork. Wrap in heavy-duty aluminum foil. Preheat grill to medium heat and grill for at least 45 minutes or until fork tender. Use caution when opening the foil to avoid burns.

To grill spears*, peel and cut the sweet potatoes lengthwise into eight spears each. Set potatoes, skin side down, on a plate or baking sheet; brush cut sides with oil. Preheat grill to medium heat and grill cut sides down, about 8 minutes, turning often, until lightly charred in spots and cooked through.

To grill fries*, peel sweet potatoes and slice into ½ x ½" sticks. Brush all sides with oil. Preheat grill to medium heat and grill until browned on all sides. Remove from heat and sprinkle with desired seasonings.

To grill slices*, peel and slice sweet potatoes. Slicing them very thin will result in a crisp "chip", while the end result of thicker slices will be a bit more tender in the middle and crispy on the outside. Oil the grate lightly and preheat grill to medium heat. Place the slices directly on the grate and grill approximately 5 to 10 minutes, depending on thickness. Turn once halfway through cooking time.

To grill in foil*, peel sweet potatoes and cut into cubes. Coat a double thickness of heavy-duty aluminum foil with nonstick cooking spray. Make the foil large enough to fold up around the potatoes, leaving some room for air circulation. Add sweet potatoes in an even layer; top with several teaspoons of butter or drizzle with oil. Sprinkle with seasonings, if desired, and cook on grill with lid closed until tender, about 40 minutes.

* Variation: Sweet potatoes can be parboiled before grilling to cut down on grilling time. Just simmer in hot water until nearly tender, but still sturdy.

By selecting sweet potatoes that are firm to the touch with a relatively smooth exterior surface, you'll be well on your way to creating the sweet spuds of your dreams.

CILANTRO DIPPING SAUCE

Makes about 2 cups

1 C. plain yogurt
½ C. sour cream
1 fresh jalapeño or other hot chile pepper
¼ C. chopped fresh cilantro
2 T. grated onion
3 T. salsa

In a medium bowl, stir together yogurt and sour cream until smooth. Add chile pepper, cilantro, onion and salsa. Stir until well blended; cover with plastic wrap and refrigerate for at least 15 minutes before serving with grilled sweet potatoes.

SOUR CREAM DIPPING SAUCE

Makes about ¾ cup

¾ C. sour cream
2 tsp. lime juice
1 tsp. chopped fresh parsley
¼ tsp. minced garlic
¼ tsp. ground cumin
¼ tsp. salt
⅛ tsp. finely grated lime peel
1 canned chipotle pepper in adobo, minced, optional

Combine sour cream, lime juice, parsley, garlic, cumin, salt and lime peel. Stir well. Add chipotle pepper for more kick, if desired. Serve dipping sauce with grilled sweet potatoes.

HONEY SESAME DIPPING SAUCE

Makes about 1 cup

¼ C. soy sauce
¼ C. rice vinegar
3 T. honey
2 T. finely chopped green onion
2 T. toasted sesame seeds*
1 T. toasted sesame oil

In a small bowl, combine soy sauce, vinegar, honey, onion, sesame seeds and oil. Stir until honey dissolves. Serve dipping sauce with grilled sweet potatoes.

* To toast sesame seeds, heat the seeds in a dry pan over medium heat on the grill or stovetop or on a baking sheet in a 275° oven, until golden and fragrant, about 5 minutes. Watch carefully as seeds brown quickly and continue to brown after they are removed from the heat.

Dunk your sweet spuds into one of these dipping sauces for a complementary flavor companion.

CREAMY CHIVE DIP

Makes about 1 cup
½ C. sour cream
½ C. mayonnaise
2 T. chopped fresh chives
1 tsp. steak seasoning
2 T. grated Parmesan cheese

In a small bowl, combine sour cream, mayonnaise, chives and seasoning. Stir in cheese and serve with grilled sweet potatotes.

BASIC GRILLED SWEET POTATOES

Makes 4 servings
2½ T. butter or margarine, melted
¼ tsp. salt
1½ lbs. sweet potatoes
Toasted shredded coconut*, optional

In a small bowl, mix butter and salt. Follow instructions for preparing and grilling spears, fries or slices on page 126, brushing frequently with butter mixture during grilling. Sprinkle with coconut at serving time, if desired.

* To toast coconut, place in a dry pan over medium heat on the grill or stovetop or on a baking sheet in a 350° oven for about 10 minutes, stirring occasionally to brown evenly.

SUGARED SWEET POTATOES

Makes 4 servings
2½ T. butter or margarine, melted
3 T. brown sugar
1 tsp. ground cinnamon
1½ lbs. sweet potatoes
Toasted shredded coconut*, optional

In a small bowl, mix butter, brown sugar and cinnamon. Follow instructions for preparing and grilling spears, fries or slices on page 126, brushing frequently with butter mixture during grilling. Sprinkle with coconut at serving time, if desired.

* To toast coconut, place in a dry pan over medium heat on the grill or stovetop or on a baking sheet in a 350° oven for about 10 minutes, stirring occasionally to brown evenly.

Give the basic recipe a try and then branch out and experience the difference a few "add-on" seasonings or glazes can make.

Sweet Potatoes

VEGETABLES

SPICY SWEET POTATOES

Makes 4 servings
¼ tsp. salt
½ tsp. ground cumin
½ tsp. paprika
¼ tsp. ground cinnamon
¼ tsp. chipotle powder
1 T. apple cider vinegar
2 T. olive oil
1½ lbs. sweet potatoes

In a small bowl, mix salt, cumin, paprika, cinnamon, chipotle powder and vinegar. Add oil slowly.*

* Follow instructions for preparing and grilling spears, fries or slices on page 126, brushing frequently with butter or oil mixture.

GARLIC & HERB SEASONED POTATOES

Makes 4 servings
2½ T. olive oil
3 cloves garlic, finely chopped
1 tsp. minced fresh thyme
⅛ tsp. red pepper flakes
1 T. minced parsley
1½ lbs. sweet potatoes

In a small pan, heat oil. Add garlic, thyme, red pepper flakes and parsley; cook until garlic is just soft. Remove from heat.*

* Follow instructions for preparing and grilling spears, fries or slices on page 126, brushing frequently with butter or oil mixture.

HONEY GLAZED POTATOES

Makes 4 servings
¼ C. honey
¼ C. butter, softened
1½ lbs. sweet potatoes

In a small bowl, mix honey and butter. Follow instructions for preparing and grilling spears, fries or slices on page 126, but brush with butter mixture immediately before the potatoes are turned; then glaze the other side.

SWEET POTATOES 'N' APPLES

Makes 4 servings

4 large baking apples, peeled, cored
   and sliced
4 medium sweet potatoes, peeled and sliced
1 tsp. ground cinnamon
2 T. sugar
4 T. butter
½ C. miniature marshmallows

Preheat grill to medium heat. In a large bowl, combine apples, sweet potatoes, cinnamon and sugar. Divide mixture into four equal portions, placing each on a large piece of heavy-duty aluminum foil sprayed with nonstick cooking spray. Top each with an equal amount of butter and marshmallows. Seal foil around each portion and grill about 40 minutes with lid closed.

Variation: Parboil sweet potatoes until tender. Peel and mash. Add butter and sugar, mixing well. Scoop out inside of apples, leaving a ¼" thick shell. Stuff the apples with sweet potato mixture. Top with marshmallows and wrap each in aluminum foil, sealing tightly. Close lid and bake on a medium-hot grill for about 15 minutes.

GLAZED SWEET POTATO PACKETS

Makes 4 servings

2 large sweet potatoes, peeled and sliced
⅓ C. orange marmalade
¼ C. brown sugar
½ tsp. ground cinnamon
1 T. butter, melted

Divide sweet potatoes evenly among four sheets of heavy-duty aluminum foil. In a small bowl, combine marmalade, brown sugar, cinnamon and butter; spread over sweet potatoes. Bring up sides of foil and double-fold top and ends to seal, leaving room for heat circulation inside. Preheat grill to medium heat. Grill 30 to 40 minutes or until tender.

PECAN-GLAZED SWEET SPUDS

Makes 4 servings

4 medium sweet potatoes
½ C. pecan halves
½ C. brown sugar
¼ C. butter

Parboil sweet potatoes until tender. Cut into ½" slices. Place slices on heavy-duty aluminum foil and arrange pecans on top. Sprinkle with brown sugar and dot with butter. Bring up sides of foil and double-fold top and ends to seal, leaving room for heat circulation inside. Bake on preheated hot grill for about 20 minutes.

FRUITS

BASIC COOKING TIPS

Fruits are fantastic and easily made on the grill. That means entire meals—from start to finish—can be prepared outside. Grilling tends to bring out the natural sugars in fruit—although you can never go wrong by adding a sweet or savory glaze. There are very few fruits that cannot be put on the grill. Even those that appear to small or thin can be threaded on skewers, wrapped in foil or put in a grill basket. Clean the grates well before cooking sweets. You don't want your pineapple to taste like a ribeye.

APPLES & PEARS

To grill whole apples or pears, remove core from each piece of fruit without cutting through to the bottom, forming a cavity. Preheat grill to medium heat. Set fruit cored-side-up on heavy-duty aluminum foil. Add 1 teaspoon butter and a sprinkle of cinnamon and sugar to each cavity or stuff with filling. To grill, wrap securely in aluminum foil, folding ends over, leaving a little space for air circulation. Grill, seam side up, about 10 minutes or until fruit is slightly tender.

To grill rings of fruit, remove stem and blossom ends and slice the remainder of the fruit into crosswise slices, about ½" thick, removing seeds and core. Preheat grill to medium heat. Place rings, cut side down, directly on grate or use a grill basket. Grill until lightly browned. Using a spatula or tongs, carefully turn rings and grill the other side until brown. Fruit rings can also be wrapped in heavy-duty aluminum foil, folding ends of foil over and leaving a little space for air circulation. Grill, seam side up, until fruit is tender.

To grill fruit halves or wedges, slice fruit in half vertically and remove core and stem. Further slice into wedges, if desired. Preheat grill to medium heat. Place cut side down on grate. Grill both sides until lightly browned, turning carefully with a spatula or tongs. Fruit can also be grilled in a grill basket or wrapped in heavy-duty aluminum foil as described above.

To grill on skewers, slice fruit in half, removing core and stem. Slice each half into chunks or thick slices and thread onto skewers*. Preheat grill to medium heat. Place skewers on grate, turning occasionally until fruit is lightly browned and softened.

* If using wooden skewers, be sure to soak in water at least 30 minutes before using to prevent burning.

Apples and pears share a common texture and mild flavor. Firmer types of fruit (Bosc pears, for example), should be used for grilling. Both apples and pears can be stuffed and grilled in foil, skewered or grilled directly on the grates.

Apples & Pears

FRUIT

BROWN SUGAR-CINNAMON FILLING

Makes 4 servings

4 apples or pears
¼ C. brown sugar or honey
4 tsp. chopped walnuts
4 tsp. butter, softened, divided
Ground cinnamon
Ground nutmeg

Core whole fruit to form a cavity. Combine brown sugar or honey and walnuts, stuffing each fruit cavity with an equal amount. Add 1 teaspoon butter to each cavity and sprinkle with cinnamon and nutmeg. Follow instructions for grilling whole fruit on page 132.

CAMPFIRE BAKED FRUIT

Makes 4 servings

4 apples or pears
½ C. dried fruits
½ C. shredded coconut
1 tsp. ground cinnamon
½ C. sugar
2 tsp. butter, softened

Core whole fruit to form a cavity; fill with dried fruits and coconut, packing it fairly tight. Mix cinnamon and sugar. Sprinkle each filled cavity with ½ teaspoon cinnamon-sugar mixture and ½ teaspoon butter. Follow instructions for grilling whole fruit on page 132.

GINGERSNAP FILLING

Makes 6 servings

5 T. butter, softened
5 T. gingersnap cookie crumbs
2 T. brown sugar
2 tsp. finely grated lemon peel
½ tsp. ground cinnamon
¼ tsp. ground nutmeg
½ tsp. ground cloves
1 T. orange liqueur
2 T. vanilla extract
6 apples or pears

In a small bowl, combine butter and cookie crumbs. Mix in brown sugar, lemon peel, cinnamon, nutmeg, cloves, orange liqueur and vanilla. Core whole fruit to form a cavity; fill each with an equal amount of the cookie mixture. Follow instructions for grilling whole fruit on page 132.

Experiment with these and the following recipes that can be used to fill either apples or pears.

Apples & Pears

FRUIT

SWEET NUT FILLING

Makes 4 servings

⅓ C. coarsely chopped walnuts
¼ C. golden raisins
2 T. maple syrup
2 tsp. brown sugar
1 tsp. finely grated lemon peel
⅛ tsp. ground cinnamon
2 T. lemon juice
4 apples or pears
1 T. butter
⅔ C. apple juice

Preheat grill to medium heat. In a small bowl, combine walnuts, raisins, syrup, brown sugar, lemon peel, cinnamon and lemon juice. Core whole fruit to form a cavity and fill with nut mixture. Set filled fruit into a 2-quart grill-safe pan and dot with butter. Pour apple juice around fruit and place pan on the grill. Close lid and grill for about 30 minutes or until tender, basting occasionally.

RED-HOT FILLING

Makes 4 servings

4 apples or pears
4 tsp. brown sugar
¼ C. red-hot candies

Core fruit and place 1 teaspoon brown sugar and 1 tablespoon candies into the cavity of each. Follow instructions for grilling whole fruit on page 132.

PEANUT BUTTER FILLING

Makes 6 servings

½ C. creamy peanut butter
1 T. butter, softened
¼ C. raisins
¼ C. miniature marshmallows
6 apples or pears

In a small bowl, combine peanut butter, butter, raisins and marshmallows. Core whole fruit and fill each cavity with an equal portion of the peanut butter mixture. Follow instructions for grilling whole fruit on page 132.

HONEY-CINNAMON GLAZE

Makes about 1 cup

1 C. butter, melted
1½ T. ground cinnamon
3 T. honey

Combine butter, cinnamon and honey; brush over fruit during grilling. Serve with any remaining sauce.

WARM BROWN SUGAR GLAZE

Makes about ⅓ cup

2 T. brown sugar
2 T. lemon juice
2 T. canola oil
1 tsp. ground cinnamon

In a small pan, heat brown sugar, lemon juice, oil and cinnamon. Brush over fruit while grilling.

LIME, CILANTRO & BLACK PEPPER GLAZE

Makes about ¾ cup

¼ C. lime or lemon juice
¼ C. honey
¼ C. chopped fresh cilantro
Black pepper to taste

In a small saucepan, warm the lime juice and honey. Stir in cilantro. Brush fruit with warm lime mixture and dust with black pepper while grilling. Serve with any remaining glaze.

BUTTER PECAN SAUCE

Makes about 1¼ cups

⅓ C. brown sugar
2 T. sugar
4 tsp. cornstarch
¾ C. heavy whipping cream
1 T. butter
½ C. chopped pecans

In a small saucepan, combine brown sugar, sugar and cornstarch. Gradually stir in cream until smooth. Bring to a boil, stirring constantly; cook and stir 2 to 3 minutes or until slightly thickened. Remove from heat; stir in butter until smooth. Add pecans. Serve with grilled apples or pears.

Try one of these delicious glazes, brushed on sliced fruit at grill time. Apples and pears are both delicious with any of these recipes. (See instructions for grilling sliced fruit or skewers on page 132.)

RASPBERRY SAUCE

Makes about 1¼ cups

1 (10 oz.) pkg. frozen raspberries in light syrup, thawed, undrained
1 tsp. lemon juice

In a blender or food processor bowl, combine raspberries (with syrup) and lemon juice; blend or process until smooth. Drizzle grilled apples or pears with sauce.

After the fruit has been removed from the grill, a great way to intensify its flavor is by serving it with one of these great-tasting sauces!

GRILLED APPLE CRISP

Makes about 12 servings

10 C. (about 8 medium) thinly sliced, peeled apples
1 C. old-fashioned oats
1 C. brown sugar
¼ C. flour
1 T. ground cinnamon
1 tsp. ground nutmeg
¼ tsp. ground cloves
¼ C. cold butter

Place apple slices on a double thickness of heavy-duty aluminum foil (about 12 x 24") which has been sprayed with nonstick cooking spray. In a small bowl, combine oats, brown sugar, flour, cinnamon, nutmeg and cloves; cut in butter until mixture is crumbly. Sprinkle over apples. Fold foil around apple mixture and seal tightly. Grill, covered, over medium heat 20 to 25 minutes or until apples are tender.

Instead of grilling just the fruit, try grilling the entire dessert! This one is baked in foil and comes out hot, bubbly and delicious.

Apples & Pears

FRUIT

GRILLED PEAR & WATERCRESS SALAD

Makes about 6 servings

2 T. brown sugar
¼ tsp. black pepper
2 T. chopped walnuts
2 pears, cored and cut into 6
    lengthwise wedges
Lemon juice for brushing
2 T. fresh lemon juice
1 T. rice vinegar
1 tsp. Dijon mustard
1 T. minced shallot
¼ tsp. salt
¼ tsp. black pepper
1 T. olive oil
6 C. watercress sprigs, tough stems removed
3 T. crumbled blue cheese

In a small pan over medium heat, combine brown sugar, 1 tablespoon water and black pepper. Cook, stirring constantly, until sugar dissolves. Stir in walnuts; reduce heat to low and cook for 30 seconds. Remove from heat and quickly spread nuts on a sheet of parchment paper or a plate. Set aside to cool. Brush the pear wedges with lemon juice and grill over medium heat until pears begin to brown, 3 to 4 minutes, turning once. Set aside. To make the vinaigrette, in a small bowl, whisk together 2 tablespoons lemon juice, vinegar, mustard and shallot. Add salt and black pepper; whisk to blend. While whisking, slowly add the oil in a thin stream until emulsified. In a large bowl, combine watercress and cheese; add vinaigrette and toss gently to mix well and coat evenly. To serve, divide the salad among individual plates. Place two pear wedges on each and sprinkle with candied walnuts.

 Grilled fruit makes an appetizing addition to other recipes. Try tossing with greens and a few other ingredients to make this unique salad.

APRICOTS, NECTARINES & PEACHES

To grill fruit halves, cut each in half, removing pit. Brush cut side with oil. Place cut side down on grate. Grill 3 to 5 minutes per side or until fruit begins to soften.

To grill on skewers, cut each fruit in half, removing pit. Cut in half again and thread fruit onto metal or wooden skewers*. Brush with oil or marinade and grill, uncovered, over medium heat for 1 to 2 minutes per side or until grill marks appear and fruit begins to soften.

To grill in foil, cut a 12" square piece of heavy-duty aluminum foil for each whole fruit. Preheat grill to medium-low heat. Cut each piece of fruit in half, removing pit. Place one piece of fruit, cut side up, on each piece of foil. Add a bit of butter and any additional toppings to each half. Fold foil around fruit and seal tightly leaving space for air circulation. Close lid and grill 10 to 20 minutes or until fruit is tender.

* If using wooden skewers, be sure to soak in water at least 30 minutes before grilling to prevent burning.

Apricots, nectarines and peaches all lend themselves well to grilling and can be used interchangeably in many recipes. However, when using apricots, you may wish to use more of them since they are smaller. No matter which fruit you use, spray a cold grill grate with nonstick cooking spray or brush lightly with oil before grilling.

FRUIT & BLUE CHEESE

Makes 4 servings

4 fresh apricots, nectarines or peaches, halved and pitted
Blue cheese
Honey
Coarsely ground black pepper

Prepare and grill fruit halves as directed on page 138, adding crumbled blue cheese to the center of each after they have been turned cut side up. Continue grilling until fruit begins to soften and cheese melts. Remove from grill; drizzle with honey and sprinkle with black pepper.

GRILLED FRUIT WITH CHOCOLATE & ALMONDS

Makes 4 servings

4 fresh apricots, nectarines or peaches,
   halved and pitted
Vegetable oil
4 oz. bittersweet chocolate, melted
¼ C. slivered almonds, toasted and chopped

Preheat grill to high heat. Prepare and grill fruit as directed on page 138. Transfer to a serving plate and drizzle with melted chocolate and sprinkle with almonds.

GRILLED HONEYED FRUIT

Makes 4 servings

4 fresh apricots, nectarines or peaches,
   halved and pitted
¼ C. honey
2 T. butter, melted
½ tsp. ground nutmeg
½ tsp. ground cinnamon

Prepare and grill fruit as directed on page 138, brushing with honey and butter after turning. Remove from grill; sprinkle with nutmeg and cinnamon.

GINGER & SPICE GRILLED FRUIT

Makes 6 to 8 servings

6 fresh apricots, nectarines or peaches,
   halved and pitted
¼ C. brown sugar
1 T. sugar
¼ tsp. ground ginger
⅛ tsp. ground cinnamon
2 tsp. lemon juice

In a large bowl, whisk together brown sugar, sugar, ginger, cinnamon, 1 tablespoon water and lemon juice. Place fruit cut side down into marinade. Cover with plastic wrap and refrigerate 2 to 4 hours. Prepare and grill fruit halves as directed on page 138.

GRILLED FRUIT 'N' BLUEBERRIES

Makes 6 servings

6 medium apricots, nectarines or peaches,
   halved and pitted
2 C. fresh blueberries
¼ C. brown sugar
¼ C. butter
2 T. lemon juice

Preheat grill to medium-low heat. Place fruit halves cut side up on 12 x 12" pieces of heavy-duty aluminum foil. Sprinkle each fruit half with some of the blueberries, brown sugar, butter and lemon juice. Fold foil around fruit and seal tightly. Close lid and grill 18 to 20 minutes or until tender.

FRUIT WITH RASPBERRY SAUCE

Makes 4 servings

1 (10 oz.) pkg. frozen raspberries in syrup, slightly thawed
1 T. lemon juice
4 fresh apricots, nectarines or peaches, peeled, halved and pitted
3 T. brown sugar
½ tsp. ground cinnamon
1 tsp. vanilla extract
2 tsp. butter

In a blender or food processor bowl, process raspberries and lemon juice until pureed. Strain and discard seeds, if desired. Cover and chill. Preheat grill to medium heat. Place fruit halves, cut side up, on 12 x 12" double-thick pieces of heavy-duty aluminum foil. Combine brown sugar and cinnamon; sprinkle into peach centers. Sprinkle each with some vanilla and dot with some of the butter. Fold foil over peaches and seal. Grill 15 minutes or until heated through. Serve with raspberry sauce.

FRUIT 'N' CAKE KEBABS

Makes 8 servings

½ C. apricot preserves
1 T. butter
⅛ tsp. ground cinnamon
⅛ tsp. ground nutmeg
3 nectarines, pitted and quartered
6 medium apricots, pitted and halved
3 medium peaches, pitted and quartered
1 (10¾ oz.) loaf frozen pound cake, thawed and cut into 2" cubes

Preheat grill to medium heat. In a small saucepan over medium heat, blend preserves, 1 tablespoon water, butter, cinnamon and nutmeg. On eight skewers*, alternately thread fruit and cake. Grill, uncovered, for 1 to 2 minutes on each side or until cake is golden and fruit is tender, brushing often with apricot mixture.

FRUIT & CHOCOLATE SAUCE

Makes 6 servings

¾ C. semi-sweet chocolate chips
¼ C. butter
⅔ C. sugar
1 (5 oz.) can evaporated milk
2 peaches, pitted and cut into wedges
2 bananas, peeled and cut into 1" chunks
6 strawberries, stemmed

In a small saucepan over low heat, melt chocolate and butter. Add sugar. Gradually stir in milk. Bring to a boil; reduce heat and cook, stirring constantly, about 8 minutes. Set aside. Preheat grill to medium heat. Alternately thread fruit onto skewers*. Grill for about 5 minutes, turning once. Remove from grill and serve with warm chocolate sauce.

* If using wooden skewers, be sure to soak in water at least 30 minutes to prevent burning.

BANANAS

To grill bananas in their skins, leave whole, slice in half horizontally or cut through the top of the peel and banana without cutting through the bottom. If whole, just place on a grill preheated to medium heat with lid closed, grilling for about 3 to 5 minutes, turning occasionally. If cut, place on a grill preheated to medium heat and grill, cut side up, closing the lid and grilling until bananas begin to pull away from the peel, 3 to 5 minutes. Cutting allows you to easily stuff with filling. The fruit will be soft, so remove carefully from peels.

To grill without skins, place whole or cut bananas in a foil pan or on heavy-duty aluminum foil. Preheat grill to medium heat. Fold foil around bananas but do not seal or cover pan. Grill for about 10 minutes or until bananas are tender.

To grill on skewers, cut bananas into 1½" chunks. Thread onto skewers*, brush with oil or butter and add spices, if desired. Preheat grill to medium heat and grill for about 5 minutes on each side, brushing occasionally with oil or butter. Do not overcook.

* If using wooden skewers, be sure to soak in water at least 30 minutes before using to prevent burning.

GRILLED BANANAS

Makes 6 servings

6 firm, ripe bananas, unpeeled and
   halved lengthwise
⅓ C. honey
¾ C. brown sugar

Place the banana halves (still in their peel), cut side up on a plate and drizzle evenly with honey. Sprinkle with brown sugar and transfer bananas to the grill, cut side up. Follow grilling instructions above.

BACON MAPLE BANANA BITES

Makes 8 servings

2 large bananas
1 tsp. chili powder, or to taste
¼ C. maple syrup
8 strips center-cut bacon

Lightly oil or spray grates with nonstick cooking spray. Preheat grill to medium heat. Pour maple syrup into shallow dish; place bacon on a microwave-safe plate lined with paper towels. Cover with another paper towel and microwave on high 1 minute or until bacon just begins to cook, but is still pliable. Peel bananas and sprinkle with chili powder; cut each into four equal pieces. Roll pieces in maple syrup and wrap in one strip of bacon. Secure with toothpicks. Place on grill, close lid and heat 5 to 8 minutes or until bacon is browned and crisp, turning occasionally.

FRUIT KEBABS

Makes 6 servings

5 firm bananas, peeled
1 small cantaloupe, seeded and
   rind removed
12 large firm strawberries, stemmed
¼ C. butter, melted
2 T. fresh lime juice
1 T. honey

Preheat grill to medium heat. Cut bananas and cantaloupe into 1½" chunks. Thread on skewers alternately with strawberries. Combine butter, lime juice and honey; brush kebabs with mixture and place on grill. Cook about 5 minutes on each side, brushing occasionally with butter mixture. Serve immediately.

* If using wooden skewers, be sure to soak in water at least 30 minutes before using to prevent burning.

BANANA BOATS

Makes 4 servings

4 bananas, unpeeled
¼ C. semi-sweet chocolate chips
½ C. chopped strawberries
⅓ C. granola or graham cracker crumbs
½ C. miniature marshmallows
¼ C. chopped walnuts

Preheat grill to medium heat. Cut lengthwise through the top of the peel and banana without cutting through the bottom. Arrange each banana on a piece of heavy-duty aluminum foil. Gently pry open each banana. Sprinkle chocolate chips, strawberries and granola down the center of each banana; top with marshmallows and nuts. Fold foil around the sides of each banana, leaving the top open. Grill until marshmallows are melted, about 10 minutes. Cool slightly before serving.

Take bananas from plain to sensational!

Bananas

FRUIT

CHOCOLATE BANANA PEANUT BUTTER CUPS

Makes 4 servings

4 miniature graham cracker pie crusts
1 banana
12 miniature peanut butter cup candies
1 C. miniature marshmallows

Preheat grill to medium heat. Place pie crusts in a disposable foil pan. Peel and slice banana, and layer 3 to 4 slices in each pie crust. Place 3 peanut butter cups over top of bananas. Sprinkle about ¼ cup marshmallows over the top of each. Cover pan with aluminum foil and place on grill for 10 to 15 minutes.

SPICED GRILLED BANANAS

Makes about 4 servings

3 large, firm bananas, peeled
¼ C. golden raisins
3 T. brown sugar
½ tsp. ground cinnamon
¼ tsp. ground nutmeg
¼ tsp. ground cardamom or coriander
2 T. butter, cut into 8 pieces
1 T. fresh lime juice
Frozen vanilla yogurt
Additional fresh lime juice

Preheat grill to low heat. Spray 9" disposable foil pan with nonstick cooking spray. Cut bananas diagonally into ½" thick slices. Overlap in prepared pan. Sprinkle with raisins. In a small bowl, combine sugar, cinnamon, nutmeg and cardamom; sprinkle over bananas and raisins. Dot with butter. Cover pie plate tightly with foil. Place on grate, close grill lid and cook over low heat 10 to 15 minutes or until bananas are hot and tender. Carefully remove foil and sprinkle with lime juice. Serve over frozen yogurt and sprinkle with additional lime juice.

Bananas

FRUIT

PINEAPPLE

To grill pineapple wedges, cut bottom and top off pineapple; stand up on end and slice downward, rotating pineapple, until outer skin is completely removed. Slice pineapple, from the top down around core to create long thick wedges. Preheat grill to medium heat. Brush wedges with oil, glaze or marinade and place on grill that has been preheated to medium heat until browned grill marks form. Turn wedges over and grill until all sides are browned.

To grill pineapple slices, remove outer skin from pineapple as directed above and cut into ½" slices or rings. Brush with oil, glaze or marinade and place on grill that has been preheated to medium heat. Grill until nicely browned on both sides.

To grill on skewers, cut pineapple wedges or slices into chunks and thread onto skewers*. Brush with oil, glaze or marinade, if desired, and again, grill until evenly browned on all sides.

To grill in aluminum foil, place pineapple in heavy-duty aluminum foil (or in a foil pan covered with foil) sprayed with nonstick cooking spray. Add sauces, marinades or olive oil, if desired. Preheat grill to medium heat. Using indirect heat, grill for 5 to 10 minutes until tender. Grilling in foil produces a softer texture than grilling directly on the grate.

* If using wooden skewers, be sure to soak in water for at least 30 minutes to prevent burning.

Grilling pineapple brings out its sugars and creates a wonderfully sweet treat to eat alone or along with other foods. If you haven't tried grilling this tropical fruit, be sure to add it to your "To Do" list.

Pineapple

FRUIT

HONEY-LIME MARINADE

Makes enough for one pineapple

1 T. olive oil
¼ tsp. ground cloves
1 tsp. ground cinnamon
2 T. honey
1 T. fresh lime juice
1 T. rum* or pineapple juice, optional
1 T. finely grated lime peel

In a large bowl, whisk together oil, cloves, cinnamon, honey and lime juice. Add pineapple; stir to coat. Marinate for about 30 minutes. Preheat grill to medium heat; grill pineapple for 3 to 4 minutes, basting occasionally. Turn the fruit and move it to a cooler part of the grill or reduce heat. Baste again and grill until pineapple is tender and golden, about 3 minutes. Remove from grill. Brush with rum or pineapple juice, if desired, and sprinkle with lime peel.

PIÑA COLADA MARINADE

Makes enough for one pineapple

¼ C. canned coconut milk
2 to 3 tsp. ground cinnamon
½ C. sugar

Place milk in a small bowl. In a separate small bowl, combine sugar and cinnamon. Coat pineapple with milk; then roll in cinnamon-sugar mixture. Grill for about 6 minutes on each side.

BROWN SUGAR MARINADE

Makes enough for one pineapple

½ C. brown sugar
¼ C. rice vinegar
¼ C. rum* or pineapple juice
3 T. lime juice

In a small bowl, stir together brown sugar, vinegar, rum and lime juice until sugar dissolves. Pour mixture over pineapple and set aside for approximately 30 minutes. When ready to grill, drain pineapple, reserving brown sugar mixture. Grill over medium heat 6 to 8 minutes, turning once, and brush occasionally with reserved sugar mixture.

* Use caution as alcohol can cause flare-ups.

Pineapple

FRUIT

CHERRY-HONEY MARINADE

Makes enough for one pineapple
3 T. honey
¼ C. cherry brandy*
2 tsp. lemon juice

In a nonporous glass dish or bowl, combine honey, brandy and lemon juice. Add pineapple to marinade; stir to coat. Cover dish and refrigerate 1 hour. Remove pineapple from dish, discarding any leftover marinade. Grill on both sides until grill marks are golden brown.

* Use caution as alcohol can cause flare-ups. A combination of ¼ cup apple juice plus 1 tsp. cherry extract can be used in place of the cherry brandy.

GINGER CREAM SAUCE

Makes enough for one pineapple
½ C. sour cream
1 T. brown sugar
1 T. chopped crystallized ginger
6 maraschino cherries

Mix sour cream, brown sugar and ginger. Cover and refrigerate until serving time. Top grilled pineapple with sauce and garnish with cherries.

Pineapple

FRUIT

INDEX

Recipe Index by Title

Recipe Index by Main Ingredient and Preparation Method

PORK

SEAFOOD

VEGETABLES

FRUITS

More Great Books from Fox Chapel Publishing

Easy Campfire Cooking
200+ Family Fun Recipes for Cooking Over Coals and in the Flames with a Dutch Oven, Foil Packets, and More!
Edited by Peg Couch

Whether you are heading out on a camping trip or simply enjoying a backyard bonfire, this book will satisfy your appetite and provide hours of entertainment for the whole family.

ISBN: 978-1-56523-724-7
$12.95 · 128 Pages

The Paddling Chef, Second Edition
A Cookbook for Canoeists, Kayakers, and Rafters
By Dian Weimer

Paddler Dian Weimer shows hungry readers how to pack, carry, and cook outdoor meals that help make water borne trips memorable—for all the right reasons.

ISBN: 978-1-56523-714-8
$16.95 · 184 Pages

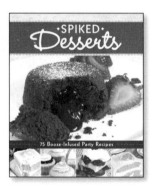

Spiked Desserts
75 Booze-Infused Party Recipes
Edited by Peg Couch

From martinis and daiquiris to grasshoppers and tequila sunrises, you can turn your favorite cocktail into an intoxicatingly delicious treat for your next adult party.

ISBN: 978-1-56523-722-3
$14.95 · 136 Pages

Edible Party Bouquets
Creating Gifts and Centerpieces with Fruit, Appetizers, and Desserts
Edited by Peg Couch

Perfect for gift-giving or any celebration, these 40 homemade, edible centerpieces are easy-to-make, inexpensive, and beautiful.

ISBN: 978-1-56523-723-0
$14.95 · 128 Pages

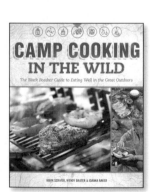

Camp Cooking in the Wild
The Black Feather Guide to Eating Well in the Great Outdoors
By Mark Scriver, Joanna Baker, and Wendy Grater

Camp Cooking can help you create a menu, set up a kitchen in the woods, and teach you new techniques and recipe ideas whether you are a beginner or a more experienced camper.

ISBN: 978-1-56523-715-5
$19.95 · 216 Pages

Treasured Amish & Mennonite Recipes
627 Delicious, Down-to-Earth Recipes from Authentic Country Kitchens
Published in Cooperation with the Mennonite Central Committee

Bring these authentic Amish and Mennonite recipes into your kitchen— includes classics like chicken pot-pie and mashed potatoes.

ISBN: 978-1-56523-599-1
$19.95 · 336 Pages